CONCILIUM

Religion in the Seventies

Concilium 121 (1/1979): Sociology of Religion

THE FAMILY
IN CRISIS OR IN
TRANSITION

A Sociological and
Theological Perspective

Edited by
Andrew Greeley

THE SEABURY PRESS / NEW YORK

1979
The Seabury Press, 815 Second Avenue, New York, N.Y. 10017
ISBN: 0-8164-2201-X (pbk.)   0-8164-0411-9

T. & T. Clark Ltd., 36 George Street, Edinburgh EH2 2LQ
ISBN: 0-567-30001-3 (pbk.)

Library of Congress Catalog Card Number: 79-65692
Printed in the United States of America

CONTENTS

Part I
Social Science

Part II
Theological Response: The Quest for Intimacy

Editorial

THIS ISSUE of *Concilium* follows the paradigm set down in earlier Sociology of Religion issues, a section devoted to the sociological data followed by a section to theological response. In the case of this issue on the family, the theological response was much easier to come by than the sociological data. Two comments seem appropriate by way of introduction.

1. There is considerable slippage in preparing an issue of *Concilium* between the original plan and the final form of the issue. In describing the issue in the preliminary 'project', I pleaded with my non-North American colleagues to provide names of scholars, both sociological and theological, who could write the articles. A substantial number of names were indeed provided but, unfortunately, most of those who were invited to submit articles for one reason or another were unable to do so. It was therefore necessary to fall back on North American colleagues with whom I had direct and immediate access. I certainly do not feel any need to apologise for an issue of *Concilium* which includes such names as Ryan, Tracy, Shea, Murphy, Sullivan and McCready; I simply would have preferred more non-North American, non-Chicago and non-Irish names. If so many Chicagoans are represented in this issue, it is despite very considerable efforts on my part to get contributions from other scholars.

In addition, there are a number of articles that I tried desperately to get and was simply unable to find an author anywhere who would write them, especially articles on the Catholic theory of intimacy and family that could be derived from folklore and from sacramental rituals. These are, it seems to me, important sources of material for theological reflection. Unfortunately, it proved impossible to obtain such articles.

2. It will be noticed that the empirical sociologists, Ryan, McCready, Sullivan, are much more hopeful about the future of the family than some of their non-empirical counterparts. Things are never quite as bad as armchair experts might think (or would like to think). Thus, for all the talk about the decline of the nuclear family, it is still true that four out of every five Americans who are married have never been divorced. One very much doubts that the rate is different in other parts of the world. As Sullivan points out in her paper, much of the changing atmosphere of family life can be accounted for by demographic transformations and not by the decline of the importance of the family unit. Theologians and social

theorists who are eager to respond to the alleged decline of the family might be well advised to check their facts before penning their response.

Recent analysis carried on at the National Opinion Research Center on divorce raises some interesting points for both theologians and social scientists. Catholic divorce has increased by almost fifty per cent (from thirteen to nineteen per cent ever divorced of those who were ever married) since the early 1970s, and is now only three percentage points behind the rate for white Protestants. Is the Catholic teaching on divorce worth only three percentage points' difference from Protestants? Has indissolubility no greater impact on people's lives than *Humanae Vitae*?

Divorce has gone up rapidly in the United States in the last decade. Many have pointed to this increase as a sign of major changes in the family if not the beginning of the end of the 'traditional family'. The more modern, the better educated, the more 'progressive' are revolting against the contraints of old-fashioned family life. However, in fact, almost all of the increase in divorce is at the lower end of the economic scale—in families with income under $10,000 a year. In this category the divorce rate is twenty-seven per cent as opposed to seventeen per cent for those over $10,000. For both Protestants and Catholics in their thirties the divorce rate for the low income group is almost fifty per cent whereas for those whose income is over $20,000 a year the rate is twenty-three per cent for Protestants and ten per cent for Catholics. It is poverty, not modernization which leads to collapse of family ties. This finding suggests that both theorists and theologians would be well-advised to look at the contexts and correlates of social change before pontificating about its meaning. The rising divorce rates in the United States are not the result of 'feminism' or the 'decline of the family'; they are related to poverty—perhaps to the inability of poor families to cope with the heavy emotional demands of family life, perhaps to the fact that the poor can now obtain cheap legal aid to seek divorce.

One of the advantages of sweeping armchair theories is that they dispense one from looking at the possible social injustice which is causing change. The 'decline of the family' in the United States is mostly happening not among the affluent and empty upper middle class in New York who write about themselves as though they were the wave of history. It is happening among the poor, especially among black and Hispanic Catholics (low income divorce rate thirty-one per cent). The 'divorce revolution' is the result of poverty and oppressive welfare laws rather than any general decline of family life.

There is no adequate substitute for empirical evidence when discussing social problems. Not all theologians seem persuaded of this dictum.

ANDREW GREELEY

Part I

Social Science

Jean Rémy

The Family: Contemporary Models and Historical Perspective

IT IS by adopting an historical perspective, and thus placing them within the context of longstanding trends, that one can best understand the models of the family that compete with one another today. And by doing so one is at the same time prevented from idealising bygone situations and regarding the past as static. Where certain spontaneously held attitudes are concerned, this involves a twofold break, which is essential if one wishes to understand the origin of present-day phenomena and their probable future development. Though I am not myself an historian, I have taken questions of sociological interpretation as my guide and examined a number of different studies based on western Europe, the context within which the concrete modalities and the demands of Christian morality have taken shape.

1. AVOIDING IDEALISATION OF THE PAST

The collective memory, in some people, tends to idealise the previous generation, and the great problems are seen as beginning with ourselves, who live in an age of moral permissiveness. One glance at a few statistics will encourage a more realistic view.

In the industrialised countries, during the last century, far more women had a professional occupation than have nowadays. The Belgian experience is rather revealing from this point of view. Belgium has the advantage of being one of the first industrialised countries on the continent to have carried out systematic censuses in the modern style (see Table 1).

3

The number of women aged between fifteen and sixty engaged in active work reached sixty-three per cent in 1866. It decreased after that, until in 1947 it reached no more than thirty per cent—a decrease which can be explained in terms of industrial strife and the improvement in the standard of living. At the moment, above all in non-working-class milieux, professional activity among women is beginning to gain ground for reasons that have nothing to do with the need for economic survival. In 1961, under the influence of this second movement, the incidence of work among women increased. The two trends operate, therefore, inversely to one another and become linked, moreover, with other developments. For example, in a large industrial centre like Seraing, the working population today seeks half as many purely civil marriages as were sought in 1925, without there being a corresponding increase in Sunday Mass attendance.

If one turns to look at eighteenth-century France, in Paris foundlings represented between thirty and forty per cent of all births, according to fluctuations in the economy (see Table 2). In 1811, a law was passed which made the abandonment of children licit by legalising the practice of the *tour*, by which abandoned children were placed in the doorways of hospitals and hospices.

One could, if one wished, continue to multiply instances such as these, of an idealised and conciliatory view of the past being contradicted by a realistic image of that past and of its problems.

Table 1: Evolution of the incidence of work among women in Belgium.

Year of census	Female population aged between 15 and 60	Active female population	Active percentage
1846	1,274,513	758,250	59·49
1866	1,396,639	883,095	63·23
1930	2,649,252	992,330	37·46
1947	2,725,104	820,916	30·12
1961	2,601,194	932,825	35·85

Source: Institut National de Statistique

Table 2: Number of children abandoned in Paris in the eighteenth century

Year	Total births	Children found	Percentage of children found in relation to all births
1763	17,546	5,253	30·1
1771	17,140	7,156	41·8
1775	19,550	6,505	33·3

Source: Moheau, *Recherches et considérations sur la population de la France*, Mouton, Paris 1778, p. 280 (quoted by P. Delooz in 'La famille occidentale et l'avenir de l'Eglise, *Pro Mundi Vita*, No. 51).[1]

2. CONTINUOUS PROGRESS CALLED IN QUESTION

We have also inherited from the nineteenth century an image of continuous and unilateral progress, according to which history consists of a progressive discovery of latent values which reached their culminating point in the preceding generation. This interpretation, which attributes an abiding quality to the usages of earlier generations, encourages an ethnocentric judgment in which the different civilisations are plotted on a rising scale, with our own at the summit. This image of continuous progress, evaluated on the basis of our present aspirations, also needs to be criticised.

In this connection, let us consider the status of women and children between the late Middle Ages and the modern era, taking into account the break created after the end of the thirteenth century by the progressive reintroduction of Roman Law. In the late Middle Ages there was a definite demarcation line separating different types of family life. South of the Loire, and including the Mediterranean countries, social life was regulated by what is customarily called written law and felt more the effects of Roman Law. To the north, and influenced rather by the Celtic and Germanic traditions, were the countries where life was based on customary law.[2]

To the extent that these traditions held sway, and above all, therefore, to the north of the Loire, women and children enjoyed autonomy and public recognition. Official acts bear the signatures of the father, the mother and the eldest son; if the father died the mother acted as guardian; fiefs, even the most important, had to be passed on to women; children could attain their majority at a very early age. In the customary family the authority of the father was that of a guardian and manager. He never had complete authority either over persons or over goods.

But at the end of the thirteenth century Roman Law was introduced into the common law world. In France, at the death of Philippe le Bel, the University of Paris discovered the fundamental law: the crown cannot be passed on through a woman, and by the seventeenth century, there was no longer any question of crowning the Queen. Women were progressively excluded from public life. They became juridically powerless. A woman's acts were null and void unless authorised by her husband. The age at which children attained their majority was progressively postponed. The family adopted the personality of one of its members: the father, who became by degrees the *pater familias* of Roman Law, a proprietor with control over persons and goods.

This resurgence of Roman Law, which was linked to the erosion of the feudal system, was supported in the market towns, which were its most important source of affirmation, and in them one can observe the gradual emergence of the bourgeois family. 'This resurgence of Roman Law occurred very early in Italy, where, moreover, there was a marked preponderance of towns from the fourteenth century onwards. It had a profound effect in the Germanic countries, where Roman Law was adopted as the common law from the middle of the thirteenth century. The Anglo-Saxon countries, on the other hand, only experienced the after-effects of it considerably later on.'[3] Having come to predominate in France at the end of the *ancien régime*, this authority was to have its seal set on it with the elaboration of the Code Civil, which in no way constituted a rupture from this point of view. It contributed to the establishment of the bourgeois family, the diffusion of which was to go hand-in-hand with the diffusion of the French Code Civil, notably in the countries of eastern Europe.

This opposition between the customary family and the bourgeois family demonstrates the non-linear character of evolution in this connection, as well as the relationship between conceptions of family life and the global problems of society where two modes of life and production clash with one another. That one comes to predominate over the other presupposes a modification of the accepted patterns of daily life.

3. THE GROWTH OF THE AUTONOMOUS FAMILY AND THE EDUCATIVE FUNCTION
OF THE PARENT-CHILD RELATIONSHIP

In Europe, particularly northern Europe, the majority of families in the Middle Ages were restricted in form, in contrast to the extended family, in which several families linked by ties of kinship live together. A number of forms of family life existed side by side in proportions which varied from place to place.[4] Those groups which were involved in the development of trade had a greater tendency than others to structure themselves according to the restricted pattern. In rural areas, the restricted family was most commonly found among the less privileged classes; as power increased so did the proportion of composite families.

But this restricted family does not correspond to the reality with which we are familiar today. It constituted a complex environment, which is nevertheless not to be confused with the extended or patriarchal family.[5] It was a combination of relatives, friends and servants. The members of a household or home lived under one roof and shared a certain number of activities. Marriage was an act of considerable importance which signified the creation of a new economic unit. It meant the addition of a new cell to the fabric of village society, the importance of which was gauged principally in terms of the number of homes it contained. Thus the poorer the milieu to which one belonged, the more likely one was to marry late. 'Its function was not at first to cherish and educate. It did not by itself alone ensure the socialisation of the child.'⁶ Its function was one of continuity, and it ensured the organisation of daily life and the protection of honour. But it was not for all that a self-contained unit.

The group in which the child lived and from which he chose his friends, was much larger than the family. The family, moreover, was not itself shut off from the surrounding milieu which penetrated into it. For the notion of private life has scarcely any more meaning here than the distinction between social life and professional life. This is obvious from their whole concept of housing. Up until the seventeenth century, the large house contained no functional divisions, and the inter-connecting rooms and absence of a corridor made any sort of intimacy impossible. When the bedroom came to be separated off from the rest, it retained its public character. The bed was the rich man's showpiece: one received one's visitors in bed and carried on a number of activities there.⁷ The houses of the working classes often amounted to nothing more than a single room, and social life went on in the village, on the farm or in one's master's house. Very young children shared the world of their elders and formed part of an all-inclusive community which might be that of the hamlet, the village, the street or the quarter and in which the affective dimension of life was given concrete expression. Children there developed affective ties with particular adults who were not necessarily their own parents.

Nevertheless, until the seventeenth century, apprenticeship was the lot of all young men, and no one escaped from it. Children were frequently sent at a very early age to another family, in order to live there and learn, according to the social class to which they belonged, good manners or a trade or Latin literature. 'The more prosperous the family was, the more numerous it was. . . . Only a small group at the middle of the scale was able to remain unaffected by these exchanges of persons as domestics.'⁸ 'At that time affectivity was not the necessary condition for the formation, continuance and stability of the family.'⁹ Except among the working classes, the sentimental element played little part in one's choice of a partner. Economic considerations predominated. If love sometimes developed after the marriage, it was not what gave it meaning in the first place.

With the growth of the merchant society, the family became progressively further removed from the milieu surrounding it and established itself as a closed economic unit. In the eighteenth century, social life, professional life and private life were more effectively separated in the large families. Each was accorded its own appropriate space: the drawing room, the study and the bedroom. Meanwhile, the dense and complex social milieu in which the child lived became correspondingly poorer. One is witnessing here a falling back on the family, now the principal source of social life, which strengthened the bond between parents and

children. The family became increasingly the source of emotional security. If it failed, there was scarcely any other milieu available to substitute for it. This concentration on the family has continued to intensify
into our own day. And it is in this context that the problem of the school
arises, and that of the link between the family and the specialised environments outside it.

This preoccupation with the child probably explains the development
of an early form of birth control which predominated until the nineteen-
forties. A second type was developed later on as greater importance was
accorded the spouses as a specific couple. The shift of emphasis involved
here is a recent one, since the emotional core of the family until the end of
the nineteenth century was rather the couple of mother and child.

The child was all the more the centre of this bourgeois family as one
moves up into those social classes where there was a patrimony to be
managed and passed on to the succeeding generation. In this case, the
family settled down as a closed economic unit, where the patrimony was
regarded as a capital asset to be made the most of, even if the family did
not strictly speaking control a unit of production. This difference assumed
its full significance in the nineteenth century, when small- and medium-
sized businesses began to grow up alongside the large ones, amassing
capital from various sources. Thus French research into nineteenth-
century bourgeois families[10] reveals the existence of a large number of
meticulously kept account books. Madame kept the cook's account book
as well as her own personal one. Monsieur kept the large book for the
entire household. Of the profits listed in this large book, less than half
represent the professional profits of Monsieur; the remainder came from
personal income or property, in which Madame's dowry played an important role. Thus the wife enjoyed a certain economic autonomy *vis-à-vis*
her husband, but she did not herself audit her husband's account book.
For reasons connected with the management of the dowry, that task fell
to the lot of Madame's father. This development of the family as an
autonomous and distinct unit was independent of the fact that it was a unit
of production, and was connected rather with the fact that it was an
economic and investing unit which had to pass something on to the next
generation.

This transmission from one generation to another applied equally to
education and to the style of family life. It was a question of passing on to
the succeeding generation the values of the preceding, possibly by closing
oneself to a hostile environment. The richer a family was, the more
numerous its domestic staff. The extent of this domestic help is explained
not only by the fact that the wages were low, but also by a desire for
autonomy which sought to have everything done in the house, the
pastry-making as well as the minor dress-making, the lessons in water-

colour painting and English. This is the very opposite of the introduction of the commercial circuit into the life of the household, including the introduction of pre-cooked foods, which characterises family life today.

The development of the family as an autonomous distinct unit involved stability and juridical formalisation. The introduction of Roman Law contributed to this, and the Church too played an important part in it. For example, in the sixteenth century the churches began to lead a campaign against premarital sex.[11] Previously the engagement or betrothal carried great weight. If the Church frowned on the unblessed marriage she did not forbid it. Very often, above all in the country, the church marriage took place when the woman was pregnant, sometimes towards the end of her pregnancy. What is more, in many places intercourse took place as a kind of test of fertility. One only married the girl when she was pregnant.[12] All this implies a society in which fertility was central to the meaning of marriage. The Church, which played no part at the time of the betrothal, emphasised the sole validity of marriage and was increasingly direct in her opposition to premarital relations. This was an historic struggle which possibly still colours the Church's reactions today. A papal bull was promulgated, confirming a decree of the Council of Trent (1564), which invalidated private contracts and ordained that all marriages should be celebrated by a priest in the church of the parish where one of the partners lived. This visibility ensured the juridical security. The fight put up by the Catholic Church gives Laslett[13] a probable explanation for the difference that existed in the eighteenth century between France and England with respect to illegitimate births. This difference in no way implied permissiveness in unmarried people who did not intend to make any form of mutual commitment, for there was always the controlling force of the milieu which made couples assume mutual responsibilities in the long term.

Even in France the battle was far from being won. This attitude was not generalised outside the circles of the bourgeoisie, and it was not rare among the working classes in the nineteenth century for people to set up house together without first going to the town hall or the church. Until only recently, one of the important pastoral duties of the clergy was to try and regularise these situations. The struggle went hand-in-hand with a desire to develop the family, in working class areas, as a distinct unit in relation to the widely diffused loyalties outside it.[14] For example, in the communal housing, promoted notably by the liberal employers, they tried to see to it that the doors of the individual houses were not contiguous but as far removed from one another as possible, in such a way as to ensure the separation of the households. Thus in diverse ways the family as an autonomous economic unit gradually became more widespread, even where there was no inheritance to be managed.

4. AFFIRMATION OF INDIVIDUAL RIGHTS AND GROWING AWARENESS OF THE MARRIED COUPLE

Parallel to this tendency, which affirmed the authority of the father, there developed as part of the liberal outlook an affirmation of the right of individuals. The ascendancy of the former movement reached its peak in the nineteenth century and was characteristic of an early phase of capitalism centred on the family patrimony. The second movement gained strength progressively from the eighteenth century onwards, establishing itself during the years between 1930 and 1940 as wage-earning became universal after the great crisis and the rupture created by the Second World War.

Under the *ancien régime* a boy apprentice had scarcely any opportunity for deciding what he was going to do, for the fact that functions were distinguished meant jt was possible to draw up contracts under which the apprentice agreed to respect the following code: 'He will not frequent taverns and cabarets. . . . He will not absent himself, either by night or by day, without the permission of his master. . . .'[15] The evolution of these multiple dependencies of individuals was regarded by many as a liberation and the struggle against the paternalism of the employer continued into the nineteenth century.

While the Code Civil of the French Revolution in many respects confirmed the rights of the father, divorce was nonetheless allowed (20 December 1792) and the rights of individuals proclaimed. All this was accompanied by various disturbances, which provoked in France a traditionalist current which demanded the Restoration. Within this current, the evolution of the family, of the State and of religion seemed bound up together,[16] and it was indicative of a tendency in the nineteenth-century Church which established itself as a force of resistance to the evolution of a civilisation which it only partially controlled.[17] In this current divorce is apt to appear as the accomplice and the companion of political democracy. By decreeing that people are equal under the law, one is doing as much harm to the State as one is to the family, since one is undermining the foundations of authority. In the State as in the family there must be 'a single head from whom all order derives in order to tend towards a single interest'.[18] Besides, nothing can be founded on the isolated individual, since his existence is too short. What is needed is time and continuity. In this sense the land-owning family, rooted in the soil, corresponds fully to the model of the perfect family, for 'possession of land is the only thing which can have any stability and continuity among us'.[18] This exaltation of the rural life was to continue into the twentieth century, and among the official organs of the Church.[19] The entire movement was upheld by a desire for security and repose.

This movement reacted against a liberal current which expressed itself, at the level of the family, through an exaltation of romantic love. This had its roots buried deep in a tradition which went back at least as far as the age of courtly love, even though at that time the marital relationship and the love relationship to the lady are distinguished from one another. The mystique of courtly love affected even Christian spirituality, where the cult of the Virgin Mother gave way to the cult of Our Lady or the Madonna.[20] The sixteenth-century mystics themselves often made use of the lover-mistress relationship to express symbolically their union with God. This movement readjusted itself within the context of the rights of individuals and progressively called in question the marriage of convenience. Then by degrees came the question of the significance of the marriage itself.[21] The creation of a bond of 'friendship' between the spouses frequently appeared at the bottom of theologians' lists of the legitimate motives for conjugal relations. Gradually a transformation of outlook took place, and the word friendship was replaced by love. This transformation, as profound as it was unconscious, found support in theological circles in Germany and reached its zenith between 1925 and 1940, notably in the work of Dietrich von Hildebrand,[22] who rejected the biological approach in order to find in the conjugal act a human meaning which is the fulfilment of conjugal love. This tendency was taken up again, partially at least, in the 1951 text of Pope Pius XII. The expressions adopted in church circles do no more than fall in, with some adjustments, to a general movement which accepts the couple more and more as a human relationship within the family itself distinct from the relationship between parents and children. This afffirmation of the autonomy of the couple is something new,[23] and it all assumes added significance when one introduces the fact of the women's movement and its search for a symmetrical relationship between man and woman.[24]

The predominance of these reactions corresponds to a transformation of the wider social context, in which the stability of the family depends more on the couple's success in establishing an affective relationship. First of all there is the fact that wage-earning has become the norm, with the result that family property is less and less common. The major part of the income of the family comes directly from work which is increasingly carried on outside it. What is more, a rise in the average income of families has made the majority of them switch the focus of their concern from survival, and the security assured by relationships of mutual assistance with their neighbours, to a situation where choice is economically possible. At the present time, the family is still evaluated as a closed economic unit, but centred on choices and plans for consumption. This is, moreover, in sympathy with the general state of the economy in the industrialised countries, where consumption has replaced spending as the motive for growth. This global context leaves the way wide open for the possibilities of a model of the family as the place *par excellence* where support can be found for the choices and the development of each member in his individual career,[25] and it is all encouraged by a process of urbanisation which is even seeping into the country districts. The autonomous family nucleus is very functional in relation to an economic demand for spatial mobility which today affects more the middle and upper classes, and particularly strongly the standard of living of these levels of the population. Is it not principally among these groups that the traditional forms of the family are at present being called in question? And do not some of them go so far as to suggest that each of us needs to find a place of security and emotional stability, for which the family is one possible concrete form, but in competition with others?[26] This movement, which is inclined to establish the right of individuals to make and unmake their own lives, tends to seek for legal recognition, and it helps one to understand certain changes that have affected contemporary law.[27] Close partnership between the spouses leads to a multiplication of the situations in which they have to act together; and then each taken in isolation is powerless to perform a valid juridical act involving the community. On the other hand, there is an increase in the number of situations in which each can act in his or her own name, and a similar increase in the number of measures which protect the rights of the child against the arbitrary action of his parents. Thus it would seem that in many respects the law is not evolving towards a relaxation of responsibilities but organising itself, rather, round new systems of ideas.

5. CONTEMPORARY CONFLICT BETWEEN TWO MODELS OF THE FAMILY

The development of these various tendencies, together with their underlying sources, has some light to throw on contemporary conflict between two models of the family. In the emergent model, the two partners control the meaning of the exchange: without reciprocity, the exchange risks losing its meaning. In this line of thinking, divorce by mutual consent will be regarded as more human than divorce granted on account of serious injuries. One sees here an education in responsibility which accepts failure while attempting to minimise its effects on the children.

This approach is regarded as an aberration by those who are inspired by the other model. The latter sets greatest value on the fact that in marrying the couple enter into an exchange the meaning of which goes beyond them personally and has a community dimension.[28]

The exposition of these two models should help one to understand many contemporary differences of outlook, since they stem from two different systems of fact and evaluation. The purpose of such an analysis, which I have attempted elsewhere,[28] is to throw light on their historical origin and their close link with different social contexts. The historical dimension should enable one to place contemporary events within the framework of movements of longer term, past or future. On that basis one might begin to analyse the type of cultural transaction that is involved between the two models and the role played by the Church in that transaction.

Translated by Sarah Fawcett

Notes

Many of the ideas taken up here originated in the course of a seminar on 'Living Relationships in the Family', organised in May 1969 by the Fondation pour la Recherche Sociale, and published in *Recherche Sociale* No. 26: 'Le devenir de la famille'.

1. P. Delooz 'La famille occidentale et l'avenir de l'Eglise' *Pro Mundi Vita* No. 51, 1974.

2. These observations are inspired by R. Pernoud 'La famille bourgeoise et son évolution' *Recherche Sociale* No. 26, 1969 pp. 5-12.

3. R. Pernoud *op. cit.* p. 6.

4. Kapisch and Demonet 'A uno pane, a uno vino, la famille rurale toscane au XVe siècle' *Annales* No. 24, 1969; J. Heers *Le Clan Familial au Moyen-Age* (Paris 1974).

5. P. Ariès *L'Enfant et la Vie Familiale sous l'Ancien Régime* (Paris 1973); P. Laslett *The World We Have Lost* (London 1965) (French translation: *Un Monde que Nous Avons Perdu* (Paris 1969)); P. Laslett *et al. Household and Family in Past Time* (Cambridge 1972).

6. P. Ariès 'Le sentiment de la famille, le sentiment de l'enfance et le sentiment de la mort: Tout bouge autour de nous et depuise toujours' *Psychologie* January 1975 p. 27.

7. J. van Ussel *Sexual Unterdrückung* (Hamburg 1970) (French translation: *Histoire de la Répression Sexuelle* (Paris 1972) p. 84).

8. P. Laslett *The World We Have Lost* p. 89.

9. P. Airès *op. cit.* p. 28. The following remarks were inspired by the continuation of this text.

10. M. Perrot 'La famille bourgeoise à la fin du XIXe siècle' *Recherche Sociale* No. 26, December 1969 pp. 17-19.

11. J. van Ussel *op. cit.* p. 172.

12. *Ibid.* p. 186.

13. P. Laslett *The World We Have Lost* pp. 154-155.

14. L. Murad, P. Zyberman 'Le petit travailleur infatigable: villes, usines, habitat et intimité au XIXe siècle' *Recherches* No. 25, November 1976 pp. 197-217.

15. P. Laslett *The World We Have Lost* p. 9.

16. R. Deniel *Une Image de la Famille et de la Societé sous la Restauration (1815-1830): Etude de la Presse Catholique* (Paris 1965); R. Deniel 'La famille dans sa relation à l'Etat et à la religion chez les penseurs traditionnels de la Restauration' *Recherche Sociale* No. 26, 1969 pp. 13-16.

17. J. L. Flandrin *L'Eglise et le Contrôle des Naissances* (Questions d'Histoire) (Paris 1970).

18. R. Deniel 'La famille dans sa relation . . .' p. 14.

19. G. Guizzardi 'Structuration et transformation d'un pouvoir symbolique (autour de la civilisation paysanne)' *Acts of the 14th International Conference on the Sociology of Religion (1977)*; *Symbolisme Religieux et Séculier et Classes Sociales Lille.*

20. W. Schubart *Religion and Eros* (Munich 1966) (French translation: *Eros et Religion* (Paris 1972) pp. 157-162); Denis de Rougemont *L'Amour et l'Occident* (Paris 1939) (republished in the collection 10/18); Denis de Rougemont *L'Érotisme au Moyen-Age* (Montreal 1977).

21. L. Flandrin *op. cit.* pp. 92-94.

22. D. von Hildebrand *Pureté et Virginité* (French translation) (Paris 1937).

23. S. Lilar *Le Couple* (Paris 1963).

24. P. Delooz 'Le feminisme, les femmes et l'avenir de l'Eglise' *Pro Mundi Vita* No. 56, 1975.

25. J. Rémy, L. Voye *La Ville et l'Urbanisation* (Gembloux 1974); see 'La famille' pp. 130-136 and 'Les classes sociales' pp. 137-143; J. Rémy 'Famille et groupe de relations personnelles en milieu urbain' *Revue de l'Action Populaire*, February 1963; J. Rémy 'La famille dans la dynamique culturelle contemporaine' *Recherche Sociale* No. 26, 1969 pp. 24-32.

26. P. Delooz 'Les formes nouvelles de vie communautaire' *Pro Mundi Vita* No. 41, 1972.

27. R. Théry 'Les rôles familiaux dans le droit récent' *Recherche Sociale* No. 26, 1969.

28. J. Rémy 'Fidelité aux engagements et structure des échanges sociaux *Lumière et Vie*, November-December 1972 pp. 6-24; J. Rémy *Famille et Modèles Culturels en Conflit* (text in preparation).

Teresa Sullivan

Longer Lives and Life-Long Relations: A Life Table Exegesis

IN THE long run, as Lord Keynes said, we are all dead. But how long is the 'long run'? One implication of the theory of demographic transition is that, on the average, the 'long run' has become much longer.[1] In 1900, the expectation of life at birth for the average citizen of the world was probably 30 years. By 1968 it had become 53 years (United Nations, 1971: 32). Seventy years is an incredibly short period of time for such a dramatic increase in longevity. We are only now beginning to consider what it might mean to have yesterday's 'long run' become today's 'short run'. For most of the world, the change in the time horizon has come about so suddenly that there has been too little time to study its effects.

Uncertain life and certain death have been the themes of poets, philosophers, and priests for centuries. Fénelon asks in *Télémaque*: 'Can any man be insensible of the brevity of life?' We sense the importance of longer life, but we have received little wisdom to guide us in a world where death—though certain—is more remote. Even in our clichés, longer life has its implications. Shall we eat, drink, and be merry, knowing that the tomorrow on which we shall die is probably some years off? Or shall we diet, abstain, and exercise, in the hope of delaying death even longer? Truly, the change in time perspectives has the potential to reshape our philosophy and thought.

Surprisingly little has been done by social scientists to chart the changes that might be expected from this revolution in longevity.[2] Despite Preston's belief (1976: ix) than the decline in mortality is a more important part of the vital revolution than changes in fertility, demographers have concentrated most of their energies on fertility. From the viewpoint of formal demography, this is reasonable. Declines in mortality affect the

15

size, age composition, and sex ratio of populations, but this effect is much smaller than the effect made by changes in fertility (Coale, 1956). From the point of view of other disciplines, however, the change in life expectancies opens up two important possibilities: the possibility of planning and the option to delay some life events without forgoing them. Death under modern mortality conditions becomes more like hurricanes and violent thunderstorms with modern meteorology—still terrible and still inevitable, but somehow less threatening because predictable. Even in the secular realm, one begins to ask, 'O Death, where is your sting?'.

This paper traces some of the implications of declining mortality in three areas: the human life-cycle, marriage and families, and religious beliefs. The reasoning used is, at some points, frankly speculative. The effects of lower mortality on human institutions are imperfectly known, and the effects of very rapid changes in mortality, such as those experienced in this century, are even less well-known. Nor is Europe an adequate historical precedent, for although mortality rates began to fall in Europe several centuries ago, the decline was very gradual and is confounded with the processes of industrialisation and urbanisation. Even in today's developing countries, declining mortality may occur simultaneously with urban growth and economic development. However, development is not *necessary* for a decline in mortality. A developing country today can achieve tremendous mortality declines with only a modest expenditure for vaccines, sanitation, and famine relief. Thus the 'pure' effects of a mortality decline are not established.

THE LIFE TABLE

The life table is a statistical model used by demographers to describe the effects of mortality on a population. Life tables are computed using data from observed or simulated populations. The data reported in this paper were drawn from observed European populations, for which there was information about age at death and the age composition of the population. An assumption made in these life tables was that the observed rates of death at every age would continue indefinitely into the future for a cohort of newborn babies. Life tables are usually computed separately for males and females.

An important datum from the life table is the expectation of life, or the average remaining life for persons who have reached a given age. If we assume that stages in the human life cycle roughly coincide with specific ages, we can approximate the proportion of a cohort of newborn babies who will live through that stage of the life cycle. By combining the expectation of life from male and female life tables, estimates for the expectation of married life, the survival of children, and the prevalence of widows and orphans can be derived. These calculations are the data used in this paper.

Moving from these data to their implications is, as I mentioned above, speculative. Nevertheless, the exercise in speculation can be fruitful for outlining potential areas of research and reflection, and for alerting us to changes in human conditions that may not yet be perceived at the individual (or psychological) level.

THE HUMAN LIFE CYCLE

Important developments have been made in recent years in studying the human life cycle. But long before Erik Erikson, poets and psalmists had presented idealised life histories. Shakespeare, in *As You Like It*, writes: 'All the world's a stage, and all the men and women merely players; they have their exits and their entrances, and one man in his time plays many parts.'[3] Shakespeare lists seven stages, culminating in 'second childishness and mere oblivion'.

Through most of human history, however, relatively few ever lived long enough to reach 'second childishness and mere oblivion'. There were always those who lived the Biblical threescore and ten years, but they were the survivors of many, many more who had been born at the same time. One of the first studies of mortality, Halley's study of mortality in Breslau from 1687 to 1691, showed an expectation of life at birth of 33·5 years. Price found 30 years for Northampton, 1735-1780; Wigglesworth found 35·5 years for colonial Massachusetts; Mourgue found 23·4 years for males in Montpellier for 1772-1792. Deparcieux in a study published in 1746, found 37·5 years for French convents and monasteries. These studies are not entirely convincing. Dublin, Lotka, and Spiegelman (1949) in their landmark volume, indicate that none of these studies was done by methods that are accepted now as accurate.

Today's more accurate techniques do not, however, lead to results that are necessarily different. According to a life table drawn by contemporary techniques, the expectation of life at birth for males in Sweden in 1778-1782 was 36 years. Under this mortality schedule, of 100,000 newborn Swedish male babies, only 41,184 could expect to reach their fiftieth birthday; only 26,934 would reach their sixty-fifth birthday. (A 1965 life table for Sweden shows 91,746 survivors of 100,000 male babies at age 50, and 76,765 at age 65.)

Table 1 shows more recent expectations of life at age 20 for males in eleven European countries. These data show the increase in expected longevity for 1850-1950. Twenty-year-old men in 1850 could have expected to live to be 56 to 62 years old; by 1950, the range was 64 to 74 years. This implies that any early generalisation about the human life cycle that extended past age 60 was including people who were, at least in terms of prevailing mortality conditions, somewhat unusual. It is not surprising that in most societies, age was venerated. To be old was, in some sense, to attain eminence. And to be eminent often required longevity.

Table 1

EXPECTATION OF LIFE AT AGE 20, MALES, SELECTED EUROPEAN COUNTRIES, 1850-1950

Country	1850	1900	1925	1950
Austria	—	40·2	—	44·5
Belgium	—	42·0	45·9	44·6
Bulgaria	—	43·1	45·8	49·4
Denmark	40·1	44·5	49·5	52·8
England and Wales	39·5	41·0	46·2[b]	49·6
France	41·3[a]	41·0	42·9	48·7
Germany	—	41·2	46·7	—
Iceland	36·4	41·5	—	51·6
Netherlands	38·0	45·7	49·7	53·3
Norway	41·5	43·6	47·7	53·9
Sweden	38·6	44·8	48·5	52·8

Sources: Dublin, Lotka, Spiegelman (1949): 346-48; Keyfitz and Flieger (1968). Given year is included in a range of years for the life table.

Notes: [a] excludes Nice and La Savoie; date of life table is 1851.
[b] 1921 data.

Studies of eminent persons have shown them, for the most part, to be long-lived. We remember the exceptions: Keats, Mozart, Schubert, Alexander the Great. But Lehman's study of the eminent (1943) showed an average age at death of over 60 years for British authors and poets, and of over 65 years for great composers, mathematicians, novelists, and educators; it was even over 65 years for naval and military commanders who were born between 1666 and 1839. Eminent geologists, historians, and U.S. Cabinet members exceeded 70 years of life. My own studies of the death data given in Butler's *Lives of the Saints* showed an average age at death of 65 years for saints who were not martyrs and who were born between the years 1400 and 1600—a period that was well before the mortality decline in Europe.

The point of this discussion is not that artistic creativity, intellectual accomplishments, and sanctity are somehow linked with the biological ability to survive. Rather, these characteristics are recognised among survivors. By contrast, eminence that is based on the accident of birth, not of accomplishment, is less correlated with longevity, even though the wellborn are likely to receive the best care that a society can afford. For example, hereditary European sovereigns had an average age at death of

only 49 years. These points have important consequences for contemporary work on life cycles.

What is universally applicable about the ageing process is not yet
known. It is likely that the physical disabilities of ageing are universal.
The social and emotional experience of growing old, on the other hand,
probably depends on the proportion of aged persons and the expectations
of growing old. It is much easier to age gracefully when old age is viewed
as a rare gift and there is a relatively small number of elders to be
respected and cared for. Those who live to old age in high mortality
regimes carry with them the memory of role exemplars, the one or two
graceful elders they may have known in their own youth. It may be easy in
these circumstances to develop and maintain norms that elderly parents
are cared for in the homes of their grown children—because relatively
few parents and children will be affected.

By contrast, when the mortality regime has changed and it is far more
common for people to live into old age, the physical disabilities of ageing
may no longer be offset by social honour. Instead, the elderly may be
viewed as a burden on the social security system and medical programmes. This development is particularly devastating for the tran-
sitional generation of persons who, in their own youth, saw the few elders
treated with great respect, but find themselves among a group of older
persons that is proportionately much larger and much less respected.
Norms about the care of elderly parents, which could be enforced when
relatively few cases were involved, may be much more difficult to sustain
when nearly every married couple can be expected to have both young
children and ageing parents to care for.

An elaboration of the attitudes and behaviour appropriate for the
'aged' is likely to vary, then, depending on whether old age is a relatively
rare or a relatively common occurrence. There have been few generations
in which large numbers of survivors reached old age; there has been no
completed generation that could expect, *from birth*, that most of its
members would reach old age. This means, then, that contemporary
formulations about the developmental psychology of late middle age and
old age must be regarded as tentative. Neither the customs of high
mortality societies nor the biographies of long-lived individuals provide
sufficient data for these formulations, and contemporary research is
being done during a mortality transition.

MARRIAGE VOWS AND LONGER LIVES

Marriage vows (and other life-long vows, such as those taken by
members of religious orders and priests) are promises made ' 'til death do

us part'. The change in mortality has caused a tremendous corresponding change in the expected duration of marriages, assuming that only death intervenes to end the marriage. In reality, divorce rates and desertion have compensated for the marital dissolutions once due mostly to death.

Table 2 compares the probability that both spouses would survive twenty-five years of marriage in Sweden in 1778-82 with the same probability in 1965. The entries provide a range of 25 to 40 years for the age at marriage of the husband, and a range of 20 to 35 years for the wife. The difference between the two tables is striking. Younger couples in 1778-82 had 57 chances in a 100 to reach their silver anniversary; the 1965 couples of the same age had 93 chances in 100. For older couples in 1778-82, the chances drop to 40; in 1965, the chances drop to 75. ''Til death do us part' was far more likely to be a short-term commitment in 1778-82 than in 1965.

Table 2

PROBABILITY THAT BOTH SPOUSES SURVIVE[a] 25 YEARS OF MARRIAGE

Sweden, 1778-82, 1965

Wife's Age at Marriage	Husband's Age at Marriage			
	25	30	35	40
	1778-82			
20	·572	·526	·501	·437
25	·557	·511	·488	·426
30	·536	·492	·470	·410
35	·511	·469	·447	·390
	1965			
20	·926	·900	·868	·792
25	·915	·890	·850	·783
30	·899	·873	·835	·769
35	·874	·850	·812	·748

Source: survival rates calculated from l_x in Swedish life tables, Keyfitz and Flieger (1968): 462-63, 508-509.

Notes: [a] only death is considered here.

Another way to analyse expected marriage duration is through a life table of marriages. In this technique, the rates of marital dissolution for every five years of marriage are applied successively to a hypothetical cohort of 100,000 couples. In this case, I assumed that the husband's age at marriage was 25 and the wife's 20, and that the death rates that applied to males and females at every age in Sweden would apply to them as they passed through successive ages. It is worth noting first that of 100,000 male babies born in Sweden in 1778-82, only 56,030 would have lived to age 25. Of 100,000 female babies, only 61,064 would have lived to age 20. The survivors who got married could expect, on the average, only 15·5 years of married life before one of them died.

(This figure differs from what you might expect from Table 2. In Table 2, the probability of survival was calculated for every couple. The life table decrements a synthetic cohort of couples—that is, in the first 5 years 8 per cent of the 100,000 marriages would have ended. Only 92 per cent would have been exposed to the next 5 years, during which another 15 per cent of the original 100,000 marriages ended. Table 2 does not use successive time periods.)

By 1965 the life table for married life in Sweden looked quite different. Again, assuming husbands aged 25 wed wives aged 20, the expectation of married life was 35·4 years. But in 1965, 96,814 of every 100,000 Swedish boys would have survived to age 25, and 98,107 of every 100,000 Swedish girls would have survived to age 20.

Longer lives mean longer marriages, but they also mean that married people are likely to be widowed later in life, and that the number of orphans will be quite small. Again using life tables, I estimated that in 1778-82, 9·8 per cent of the children under 15 would have been maternal orphans, compared with 0·7 per cent in 1965. In 1778-82, 3·7 per cent of infants under one year would have had no mother, compared with only 0·1 per cent in 1965. Peacetime societies with modern mortality conditions will not usually require orphanages—at least, not for children who are truly orphaned. (Children who have been deserted or abused, or whose parents are being divorced, are a different case.)

Some observers have argued that a 35-year commitment is not a realistic one, and so divorce has come to play a role that death once played. A person about to make a fully free commitment should have some notion of how long it might be until death parts the spouses.

One must also recognise that large numbers of broken families are not really new. Under high mortality conditions, there is greater variability in all the dimensions of family composition, simply because the effect of mortality is so pronounced at every age. But in a family broken by death, the lost spouse, parent, or child is gone 'forever'. In the family broken by divorce, there is at least the possibility for a continuing relationship, although it may be more episodic than formerly.

In the high mortality regime, parents are more likely to die, leaving widowed spouses and orphaned children. But children are also more likely to die, especially during the first year of life. Of the male Swedish babies born from 1778-82, only 80 per cent would reach their first year of life. By 1965, 98·5 per cent of them would survive the first year. For female babies, the percentages are a little different: 82 per cent would have survived the first year of life in 1778-82, and 99·8 per cent survived in 1965. The drop in infant mortality, which was an important part of the decline in general mortality, was of tremendous consequence to family life.

When mortality first declines, it first means the survival of more women throughout their childbearing years, the opportunity for much higher fertility, and the likelihood that their children will also survive to reproduce at the aggregate level. This leads to rapid population growth. At the family level, it may also lead to economic hardship and other family problems. In particular, the parents of large families may have less time to spend with each child, and so the children socialise each other. One apparent consequence of this is the lower intelligence scores of children from large families. In large French and Scottish studies, the difference in IQs between the largest and smallest families was about one standard deviation. The French study and a large Dutch study found that this relationship was true even when socioeconomic status was controlled.[4]

The decline in mortality has meant that couples could complete their childbearing by the time the woman is 25 years old, and still expect to live a long life together and in the company of their children. Indeed, the companionship of adult children and their parents is possible now on a scale never before experienced. For children, knowing their grandparents becomes a more common experience, even if their mothers have postponed childbearing to a somewhat later age. For parents, it is far more common to have both their own parents and their own children alive at the same time. This is a mixed blessing, for the middle-aged parents may feel themselves pulled in two directions and financially strained to provide for two generations of dependents.

Because lower mortality permits lower fertility, attitudes toward child-rearing and child-spacing are likely to change. One example of this is in the spacing of the second child. It was believed in the 1950s that the second child should be closely spaced after the first. Indeed, respondents in fertility surveys gave as the most frequent reason for having the second child 'to keep the first-born company'. Recent research by Zajonc (1976), on the other hand, suggests that in terms of developing the intelligence of the child, this might be exactly the wrong strategy. The intelligence of the child is aided by paternal socialisation and by the socialisation by *older* siblings; and older siblings also benefit by teaching their younger brothers and sisters. This suggests that the first child should be old enough to help 'teach'. Five or six might be an appropriate age. And although the evidence is even more fragmentary, it may be that longer spaces between children contribute to parents' marital satisfaction and to their enjoyment of their children (Clausen and Clausen, 1973; Rossi, 1978: 21).

In summary, then, declining mortality affects the family through the longer duration of marriages, the lower infant mortality and the encouragement this gives to lower fertility, the possible changes in communication within the family, and the extension of the parent-child relationship into the adult years of the son or daughter. These changes provide challenges and opportunities to understand family life within a new context. Indeed, strong family bonds, in their turn, appear to be one of the factors influencing lower mortality (Kobrin & Hendershot, 1977).

LONGEVITY AND RELIGION

There were few children under the old mortality regime who had not witnessed death, either within their own families or among their neighbours. Like the children described in Luke 7:32, they may even have played funeral games and sung childish dirges. By contrast, today children and even adults have had less personal experience of death, and this is one of the reasons given for introducing courses in death and dying into the school curriculum. Indeed, one of the advantages of providing pets for children, parents are now told, is that the pet will one day die and give the child a chance to experience death.

Contemporary society is often said to be death-denying, but this may be merely one result of a lesser familiarity with death. The vicarious experience of death, and even a cult of death, is sought within some subcultural groups. This can be as relatively innocent as providing short-lived pets for children, or as far-reaching in its consequences as widespread drug addiction. The pursuit of danger—the *chance* of death—may increase as the objective probabilities of death decline.

The life-affirming and comforting aspects of religion may be less important to people who feel confident that they will live through the complete life cycle and have time to say goodbye to their friends and kin. When the goodbyes have been said, there is a closure to the relationship that might not have been possible when most deaths were sudden and many occurred to young persons. In folklore, the ghosts who come back to haunt sites are nearly always those who have died untimely deaths, or who have left unfinished business. Those who completed their work do not seem to haunt the living. By the same token, the living who have completed their farewells may no longer feel the need to contact or appease the dead, or to assuage their guilt by praying for those who died too suddenly to confer forgiveness.

On the other hand, the meaning-structure of religion is likely to become more important as an alternative to the cult of death and danger. If life had value only because of its scarcity, then longer life would not be a blessing. If life is absurd, and its major purpose is to outsmart death for as long as possible, then longer life has no meaning and no intrinsic value. If longer life means longer commitments to other persons, but these commitments are not fulfilling, then there will be no resources to maintain those commitments.

And in that case, even though longer life means that we will experience fewer deaths, it will mean no reduction in grief and pain.

Notes

1. The demographic transition refers to the change in human population from high fertility and high mortality to low fertility and low mortality. In Europe, this change took centuries to accomplish. In today's developing countries, the mortality decline has occurred very quickly, but the fertility decline has been much slower. A classic formulation of the demographic transition is found in Notestein (1945).

2. For some efforts at spelling out implications, see Ryder (1973) and Sullivan (1978).

3. *As You Like It*, II, vii, 139.

4. See Scottish Council (1949), Institut National d'Etudes Démographiques (1973), and Belmont and Marolla (1973).

Bibliography

Belmont L. and Marolla F. A. 'Birth order, family size, and intelligence' *Science* 182 (14 Dec. 1973) pp. 1096-1101.

Clausen J. A. and Clausen S. R. 'The effects of family size on parents and children' *Psychological Perspectives on Population* J. T. Fawcett (ed.) (New York 1973) pp. 185-208.

Coale A. J. 'The effects of changes in mortality and fertility on age composition' *Milbank Memorial Fund Quarterly* 34 (1956) pp. 79-144.

Dublin L. I., Lotka A. J., Spiegelman M. *Length of Life* (New York 1949).

Institut National d'Etudes Démographiques *Enquête Nationale sur le Niveau Intellectuel des Enfants d'Age Scolaire* (Paris 1973).

Keyfitz N. & Flieger W. *World Population* (Chicago 1968).

Kobrin F. E. & Hendershot G. E. 'Do family ties reduce mortality? Evidence from the United States 1966-1968' *Journal of Marriage and the Family* 39 (November 1977) pp. 737-767.

Lehman H. C. 'The longevity of the eminent' *Science* 98 (24 September 1943) p. 270.

Notestein F. W. 'Population: the long view' *Food for the World* Schultz T. W. (ed.) (Chicago 1945) pp. 36-57.

Preston S. H. *Mortality Patterns in National Populations* (New York 1976).

Rossi A. S. 'A biosocial perspective on parenting' *The Family* Rossi A. S. *et. al.* (eds.) (New York 1978) pp. 1-31.

Ryder N. B. 'Influences of changes in the family life cycles upon family life' *United Nations Economic and Social Council, World Population Conference 1974, Symposium on Population and the Family* (Honolulu 6-15 August 1973).

Scottish Council for Research in Education *The Trend of Scottish Intelligence* (London 1949).

Sullivan T. A. 'Numbering our days aright; human longevity and the problem of intimacy' *Toward Vatican III* Tracy D. *et. al.* (eds.) (New York 1978) pp. 282-294.

United Nations, Department of Social Affairs, Population Branch *The World Population in 1970* (Population Study No. 49.) (New York: United Nations 1971).

Zajonc R. B. 'Family configuration and intelligence' *Science* 192 (16 April 1976) pp. 227-236.

William McCready

The Family and Socialisation

THIS PAPER will examine the impact of family intimacy on the religious behaviour of adolescents and their religious participation and belief. The data used here are from the 1974 NORC survey of American Catholics. Questionnaires were administered to one parent and one adolescent child in each sampled family. We will begin with a brief theoretical discussion of the socialisation process and then discuss empirical models for adolescent Mass attendance, prayerfulness and hopefulness.

Religious socialisation is a process concerned with the origins of religious thoughts, sentiments, and behaviours and the extent to which these properties are transmitted through the family from one generation to the next. There have been many family process and generational studies, far too many to present here, but they can be summarised roughly in four general findings.

First, the basic orientations which define who we are in society tend to be strongly influenced by family factors. Those orientations which are more superficial, such as our opinion on some specific political issue, tend to be influenced by non-familial characteristics. Second, parental support and warmth are associated with the well-being of the child whether this is defined as personal achievement or psychological integration. Third, the evidence is that parents tend to reconstruct the family styles they knew in their family of origin without necessarily reflecting upon them. Fourth, there is a good chance that although the 'peer group' may have considerable influence on specific adolescents, it is most likely by default. That is, the family has taken a stance of 'passive neglect' rather than the peer group superseding the influence of the familial process.

The central finding, for the purpose of this present paper, is that the quality of the parents' intimate relationship has a significant impact on the efficacy of the socialisation process. Those families in which the parents have a warm and loving relationship provide a more secure base

26

for the transmission of basic value orientations, especially those concerning the importance and the meaning of life which are symbolised in religious attitudes and behaviours. Figure 1 consists of a general model or picture of the socialisation process in which the parents and grandparents influence the religious perspective of the adolescent. (It should be noted that 'Parent Prayer' and 'Parent Religious Certainty' are inserted in the general model according to the broken lines, that is, they occupy spaces adjacent to the variables which the lines point to.)

SOCIALISATION MODELS

Mass Attendance

Table 1 contains the beta coefficients for the impact of the adult variables on the adolescent variables, and the numbers reflect the strength of the association between the adult and adolescent items, controlling for all other adult variables. In other words, the coefficient of ·4– between father's Mass attendance and boy's Mass attendance means that the association between those two variables is quite strong even after the influence of the other variables in the left-hand column on boy's Mass attendance has been accounted for.

The pattern of influence on the Mass going of the boys is made up of the father's and grandfather's Mass attendance, grandmother's Mass attendance, and the intimacy of both generations. The pattern for the girls is different in that mother's Mass attendance and father's SUPPORT are present, and father's Mass attendance and the marital intimacy of the parents are absent from the explanatory model.[1] The reason that mother's Mass going replaces father's for the girls may be due to imitation of the like-sex parent, although this represents a change from patterns found in the mid-1960s. A more interesting finding is the replacement of marital intimacy with father's SUPPORT in the girls' model. The relationship between her parents is not as important for the girl as is the degree to which she has a warm, loving, and supportive father. There is a slight variation on this theme coming up in the models for socialisation in praying.

Prayer

For the boys, both father's and mother's Mass attendance have an influence on praying, as does the intimacy of their parents and their grandparents. Of particular interest is the fact that the boys' mothers have an additional impact through their SUPPORT. For the girls the situation regarding parental Mass attendance and parental and grandparental intimacy is the same, but in this instance father's SUPPORT replaces

Fig. 1

GENERAL MODEL FOR RELIGIOUS SOCIALISATION

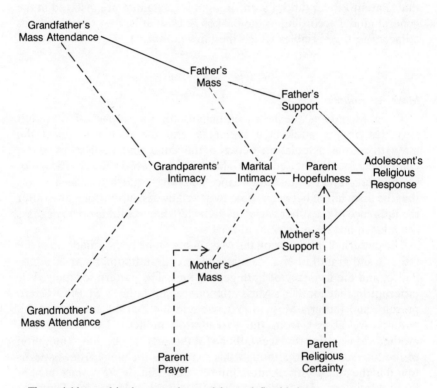

The variables used in the regression models are defined below:

Father's Mass Attendance = the frequency with which the father reported going to Mass. (In the instance where the respondent was a woman this variable is constructed from her estimation of her spouse's Mass attendance. Previous research has demonstrated that there is a high correlation between these estimates and actual behaviour.)

Mother's Mass Attendance = the frequency with which the mother reported going to Mass. (The reverse of the above construction was used.)

Marital Intimacy = the respondent's expressed satisfaction or lack of it about his/her marriage.

Mother's Support = the adolescent's perception of his/her mother as a supportive person.

Father's Support = the adolescent's perception of his/her father as a supportive person.

Grandfather's Mass Attendance = the frequency of the respondent's grandfather's Mass going, as reported by the respondent.

Grandmother's Mass Attendance = the frequency of the respondent's grandmother's Mass going, as reported by the respondent.

Grandparents' Intimacy = the happiness of his/her parents' marriage as reported by the respondent.

mother's and there is the additional influence of parental prayer. The cross-sex influence of parental SUPPORT is especially interesting when we note that prayer is one of the few religious variables which has not appreciably declined among young people during the past tumultuous decade. It may be that adolescents are particularly vulnerable to cross-sex influences due to the onset of awareness of their own sexual feelings and that prayer is tied into this in a special way. We noted in the model for the girls' Mass going that the father's SUPPORT was moderately associated with that specific religious behaviour and it may be that religiosity and sexual identity are identified, especially for adolescent girls.

Hope

Hopefulness among adolescent boys is linked to their parents' hopefulness and prayer and the certainty which the parents express when discussing religion with their children. It would appear that socialisation which produces hope in these boys is mostly due to the imitation of the parental belief system and it would be illuminating to find out more about how this particular transmission process works and why there is no comparable process for girls.

ETHNICITY AND RELIGIOUS SOCIALISATION

Here we rely on the method of selecting factors which influence a dependent variable (Mass attendance, for example) and add in factors which reduce the differences with some base comparison group until the differences are explained away. In Tables 2 and 3 the base comparison group is made up of those identifying as 'English'. In Table 2 the patterns of the ethnic groups regarding Mass attendance reveal differences in family structure effects which tie in well with our discussion of the relationship between socialisation and intimacy.

For the Irish, once parental example has been accounted for by parents' Mass attendance, there is little left to do. The other variables reduce the z-score only slightly. For the Germans, on the other hand, parental example does not have much influence, but the addition of the respondent's attitudes about sexual morality and the influence of spouse's Mass attendance account for all the decline. The Poles are like the Irish in that parental effect accounts for the difference; the Italians are like the Germans in that sexual morality and spouse's Mass attendance make all the difference.

The Irish and the Polish are most likely, then, to be affected by parental

Table 1

BETA COEFFICIENTS FOR MASS ATTENDANCE, FREQUENCY OF PRAYER,
AND HOPEFULNESS FOR ADOLESCENTS BY SEX

	Mass Attendance		Frequency of Prayer		Hopefulness
	Boys	Girls	Boys	Girls	Boys
Father's Mass attendance	·40	—	·20	·28	—
Mother's Mass attendance	—	·48	·20	·19	—
Marital intimacy	·11	—	·16	·11	—
Mother's SUPPORT	—	—	·29	—	—
Father's SUPPORT	—	·22	—	·27	—
Grandfather's Mass attendance	·12	·36	—	—	—
Grandmother's Mass attendance	·15	·28	—	—	—
Grandparents' intimacy	·14	·10	·12	·18	—
Parent hopefulness	—	—	—	—	·22
Parent frequency of prayer	—	—	—	·36	·13
Parent religious certainty	—	—	—	—	·15
Variance explained (R^2)	20%	35%	11%	26%	12%

Parent Hopefulness = the number of times the respondent gave a 'hopeful' response to the life situation vignettes concerning the death of a parent, the birth of a retarded child, a natural disaster or news that they are terminally ill.

Parent Prayer = the frequency with which the respondent prays privately.

Parent Religious Certainty = how 'sure' the respondent is when he/she speaks to their children about religion.

Adolescent Mass Attendance = frequency of Mass going reported by the adolescent respondents.

Adolescent Prayer = frequency of praying privately reported by the adolescent respondents.

Adolescent Hopefulness = the number of 'hopeful' responses to the life situation vignettes given by the adolescent respondents.

Table 2

RESIDUAL ANALYSIS FOR INFLUENCES ON MASS BY ETHNIC GROUP

	Irish	German	Polish	Italian
Raw difference from English Protestants in Mass attendance—z-scores	·13	·18	·09	−·15
Parents' Mass attendance taken into account	·04	·18	·02	−·15
Parents' Mass attendance and parents' happiness taken into account	·03	·18	·03	−·15
Parents' Mass attendance, parents' happiness, and moral attitudes taken into account	−·02	·12	·00	−·05
Parents' Mass attendance, happiness, moral attitudes, and spouse's Mass attendance taken into account	·03	·07	·00	·00

Table 3

RESIDUAL ANALYSIS FOR INFLUENCES ON FREQUENCY OF PRAYER BY ETHNIC GROUP

	Irish	German	Polish	Italian
Raw difference from English Protestants in frequency of prayer—z-scores	·09	·06	·03	−·02
Parents' frequency of prayer taken into account	·00	—	—	—
Parents' frequency of prayer and happiness taken into account	·19	·07	·08	·02
Parents' frequency of prayer, happiness, and spouse's Mass attendance taken into account	−·02	—	·02	·01

example while the Germans and the Italians are more likely to be affected by their present family variables, such as spouse's influence and their own attitudes about sexual morality.

In Table 3 the dependent variable is the frequency of the respondent's prayer. The pattern is the same for the Irish but slightly different for the other groups. Once again the Irish are influenced by parental example and to some extent by the happiness of their parents' marriage. The Germans are right on the mean and therefore show no pattern of influence, while the Poles are affected by both their parents' example and the influence of spouse. The Italians are affected entirely by the example of their parents in this matter.

These patterns of influence involving both the families of choice and origin differ from group to group and from variable to variable. In general the impact of parents is considerable, especially when we take into consideration the influence of the quality of the parental relationship. As we have seen in this last example, there is also a considerable influence exerted in some groups by the spouse. In general, this paper has been concerned with models of adolescent socialisation; but this last part indicates that there are at least two periods of socialisation, one in which the parents have a primary impact and another later on in which the spouse has a primary impact. These two stages ought to be considered in succession for a more complete picture of the process. This will be the focus of a longer paper in the future.

Finally, in Table 4 there is evidence of yet another kind of influence through the differential patterns of socialisation which we have seen in the various ethnic groups that has to do with basic world-view orientations. The data in this table are from the previously reported NORC alcohol study and consists of z-scores for hopefulness for each of the five ethnic groups. The Irish are twenty-five per cent of a standard deviation above the mean for hope and the Swedes are even higher. Both Catholic groups are above the mean while the Jews and the 'control group' (English Protestants) are below.

It is puzzling that the Irish with their problems of low SUPPORT and warmth would score so high on hope. However, in other research[2] we

Table 4

HOPEFUL Z-SCORES BY ETHNIC
GROUP

Irish	·25
Italian	·16
Jewish	−1·03
Swedish	·35
English	−·12

have noted that they are the only group to score high on trust and fatalism simultaneously, so perhaps such paradoxical behaviour is not really so surprising.

CONCLUSION

In all of the material we have discussed, the influence of family variables, especially those concerned with the quality of relationships, has loomed large. What are the implications of this, especially for those involved with the socialisation of the young into a specific value heritage such as Catholicism? There are at least three points worth mentioning: (1) the quality of the relationship between the adults in a young person's life are critically important; (2) the differences between people from different ethnic heritages are great enough to make univocal policy-making unworkable; and (3) the impact of the institutional church, with the possible exception of the Catholic school, is very little, taking these other factors into account.

The quality of the parental relationship is often a stronger predictor of adolescent behaviour than is parental behaviour itself. This may well be because children do not pay much attention to what their parents actually do, but they place great store in the way mothers and fathers act toward each other. If that relationship is successful at challenging and supporting the partners, our tentative evidence is that the children will thrive regardless of the specific example or ideology of the parents. One corollary of this is that those parents who are distanced from the church and who do not attend Mass or come into any regular contact with the formal institution may still be imparting religious values and basic orientations toward religious sensibilities to their children through the mechanism of their intimacy. The children are receiving messages about what is possible in life and what is important even though the parents themselves may be going through a time of alienation from the church.

Second, the differences between the ethnic groups and their ways of being families ought to be carefully regarded by future policy-makers and religious planners and religious educators. When the data from the alcohol study were analysed it appeared as though the Irish family was a severely troubled system. That may be, but further analysis demonstrated that the Irish were also high on hopefulness, a particularly Christian perspective (we must be doing something right!). The real lesson here is that we have to proceed with extreme caution before making judgments about the familial processes in different cultural settings and whether they are effective or not. What might appear damaging under one guise may reappear as beneficial later on. The key here is research and patience. We need to know more about the various strengths and weaknesses of these different styles of family life and we need to listen to them for what they have to tell us about the range of intimacies which are possible.

Third, the institutional church ought to shy away from specific programmes aimed at families as a whole and concentrate on developing ways to enable specific family units to build greater resources of power and support from within themselves. In order to do this we need to know much more about the needs of families and the ways in which they can be supported while at the same time not be programmed to death. One possibility is that the parish could become the locus for the initial development work. Families can be brought together in a variety of ways to support each other and to learn from each other. The institution becomes the broker rather than the authority in this activity.

It would seem from these findings that there are at least two major socialisation periods when an individual is open to being influenced in profound ways. The first is as a child in the family of origin and the second is as a spouse in the family of choice. Aside from the messages which are passed along by parents to their children, there are also messages from the parents to each other. Someone whose religious perspective and world view was not fully developed during the family of origin may have on occasion a second chance in the family of choice. What can be done to help people take the risks that are required during this period of a 'second chance'? The tradition of intimacy represented by the relationship between Yahweh and his people would seem to have a great deal to offer those seeking advice in such matters. The preliminary evidence is that these two periods of socialisation are critical for most lives. The patterns are complex and varied, the payoff often subtle and paradoxical, but the evidence also points to the conclusion that these are the best places from which to help people take the risks required for happiness; and that is where a religious institution and tradition ought to be.

Notes

1. Murray A. Straus 'Power and support structure of the family in relation to socialisation' *Journal of Marriage and the Family,* August 1964 pp. 318-326.

2. William C. McCready with Andrew M. Greeley *The Ultimate Values of the American Population* Sage Library of Social Research No. 23 (Beverley Hills 1976).

Rudolf J. Siebert

The Future of Marriage and Family: Withering Away or Restructuring?

THE AIM of this study is to explore the possible future of marriage and family in the framework of the critical theory of society as it has evolved from Georg W. F. Hegel over Karl Marx to Max Horkheimer and the Frankfurt School of philosophy and sociology.[1] Being of Judeo-Christian origin, the humanistic critical theory contributes a powerful new emancipatory impulse to the traditional and modern theological, philosophical, and sociological theories of the family. The critical theory allows for the conscious and unconscious emotional level within marriage and family without overlooking connections with wider society; family work and politics without minimising the impact of intimate communicative practice; the systematic nature of the contemporary family without excluding radically different marital and familial structures—past, present, or future. The critical theory of marriage and family is future orientated remembrance with a practical intent. It enables us to discover the dialectical logic of the development of the family and of the corresponding theological, philosophical, and sociological reflection on it in primitive, traditional, and modern society. This discovery makes it possible for us to reconstruct the developmental logic in the history of marriage and family and of their theoretical justification. On the basis of this reconstruction, the critical theory allows us to anticipate possible, probable, and desirable marital and familial forms in a post-modern society and to act toward them.

PRESENT AND FUTURE

Bourgeois futurologists tell us that industrialisation pushes primitive, traditional, and modern societies away from the concept of extended family and toward some form of the nuclear family.[2] According to the structural-functional futurologists, inevitably, societal demands for geographical mobility, increased education, or occupational specialisation are increasing the independence of women and children and undermining the theological and philosophical and practical importance of the extended family. This futurological prediction is based primarily on the continuing industrialisation of the developed modern liberal and advanced capitalistic and socialistic societies and the underdeveloped primitive and traditional societies. Should the pace of industrialisation slow down—which is very unlikely—the pressure on the extended family might decrease. But independently from the pressure of industrialisation, people still assent, particularly in organised capitalistic society, to the nuclear family pattern because it promises greater subjective freedom versus familial solidarity not only to men but also and particularly to women and children. So even if the rate of industrialisation were to diminish, the pressure of free subjectivity versus the substantiality of the family probably would not. Although this pressure alone could conceivably lead to the establishment of some form of the nuclear family as the norm in organised capitalistic society, the reevaluation of archaic, traditional, and early modern sex roles sought by feminists introduces a major doubt.[3] Such a reexamination, based on the assumption that greater subjective freedom of the particular individual versus the universality of marriage and family should be coupled with greater equality, might result in the withering away of primitive, traditional, and modern forms of marriage and family.

Structural-functional futurologists claim that a revolution in family behaviour is taking place particularly in organised capitalistic societies.[4] While from 1800 to 1950 in liberal capitalistic society positive science and technology changed rapidly but social arrangements were relatively unaffected, in advanced capitalistic society since the middle of the twentieth century, however, the locus of radical change has shifted from science and technology to social institutions, especially marriage and family.[5] In futurological perspective, family solidarity appears to be on the verge of total collapse in organised capitalistic societies, as witnessed by the steep climb of the divorce rate in the 1970s. As impossible as it may sound, 'good' marriages—measured by bourgeois standards—probably fail more often than 'bad' ones.[6] What's more, they fail precisely because they are good. The bourgeois asks too much of marriage. The marital relationship cannot produce constant heights. Good marriages seem bound to fail because, although two people may make each other happy, neither can make the other constantly ecstatic. As the bourgeois places great emphasis on self-affirmation, self-realisation, and self-actualisation of the particular subject versus the substantiality of marriage and family, he or she may never be satisfied with anything. Subjects insisting on their self-realisation as primary over against the solidarity of marriage and family are unable to overcome the paradox that success in marriage produces high-level but seemingly inevitable discontent.

According to the futurologist in Sweden today, the majority of marriages now end in divorce or separation.[7] The divorce rate has risen fairly steadily in the United States throughout the twentieth century, and recently (1977) has reached the highest level in history. The U.S.A. now has one million divorces every year. An American who gets married today faces a high likelihood that his or her marriage will eventually fail. One result of marital instability in advanced capitalistic society is that increasing numbers of children are growing up in single parent families. One out of seven American children under eighteen years of age now lives in a home without a male parent. The long term consequences of increasing marital instability remain uncertain, but they may prove extremely serious. The futurologist predicts that by the year 2000, i.e., twenty-one years from now, people will change mates even more frequently than today in advanced capitalistic society. The family will have deteriorated still further and people may have increased emotional problems unless steps are taken to offset the impact of family disintegration on children. While futurologists indicate the possibility of the family as we know it withering away, none of them anticipates the disappearing of the familial dimension as such, which leaves open the possibility of a radical renewal of this social sphere.

SUBJECTIVE FREEDOM

At an early stage of liberal capitalistic society, Hegel declares that the right of the individual subject to realise and actualise himself or herself and to be satisfied and content, or what is the same, the right of subjective freedom, constitutes the turning and centre point in the difference between the traditional societies of antiquity and modern societies.[8] In Hegel's view, Christianity—as the religion of freedom and truth— expresses in its infinity the right of subjective freedom or free subjectivity, i.e., of full self-actualisation and self-realisation of the single individual. Christianity made this right of subjective freedom into the universal real principle of a new form of the world—the modern world. The concrete forms of this Christian principle of free subjectivity are: the purpose of the eternal happiness of the individual; personal morality and conscience; the forms which on one hand arise as the principle of civil society and as moments of the political constitution of the civil state, and which appear on the other hand in modern history, particularly in the history of art, the positive sciences, philosophy and theology; and finally also the romantic love and the configuration of marriage and family characterised by this form of love.

Through Christianity, in Hegel's view, the idea has come into the world that all people are subjectively free and, as such, have the right to full self-actualisation. According to the Christian freedom message, the individual as such, man, woman, or child, has an infinite value, since he or she in his or her singularity is the object and the purpose of God's universal love. The individual subject is destined to have his or her absolute relationship to God as universal spirit and to have this divine spirit live in his or her own subjective spirit. In Christianity, man as such is called into the highest freedom. When in religion, as such, the person knows his or her relationship to God's absolute spirit as his or her essence and so finds his or her singular identity in the universal identity, then he or she has furthermore also God's spirit present as entering the dimension of wordly existence, as the divine substance of society, state, history, culture and particularly also of marriage and family. As the *real* state is an image of God's justice, so the *real* marriage and family are a reflection of God's love. Marriage and family as well as other social institutions, insofar as they do not only exist but are really real, are formed through God's spirit and are constituted in conformity to the divine spirit, just as through such existence in marriage and family and other social institutions the sentiments of social morality are internalised into the individual's subjective spirit. So the subject is really liberated in this dimension of the particular marital and familial as well as social, political and cultural existence and communicative practice.

DIALECTIC OF LOVE

At the beginning of liberal capitalistic society Hegel, who personally—like Marx and Horkheimer later on—had a very happy marriage and family life, experiences the family as immediate substantiality of man's spirit, its self-feeling unity.[9] The family has love for its essential determination. The fundamental familial sentiment consists in this, that the subject has the self-consciousness of his or her individuality in this unity of the family, which is a reality in and for itself. So in the family, the man or the woman is not only a person for himself or herself owning property, or a moral subject with private intents, or a bourgeois concerned with particular needs, drives, passions, but a familial member. For Hegel, marital love means, in general, the consciousness of my unity with the other, so that I am not isolated for myself. In love, I gain my self-consciousness only as surrender of my being-for-myself, my individuality, and through knowing myself as the unity of myself with the other and of the other with myself. This precisely is the dialectic of love. Love is feeling. As such, love is social morality in natural form. In liberal or advanced capitalistic society as production and exchange process, love is no longer present. While in bourgeois society everybody is purpose for himself, the other is either merely nothing or only a means for this particular purpose. Also, love is no longer to be found in the constitutional state. Here the citizens are aware of their unity, if at all, as the law. But the first moment in marital love is that I do not want to be any longer an independent private person for myself, a moral subject or a bourgeois, or even a citizen and that if I were such a person, I would feel deficient and incomplete. The second element in marital love is, that I gain myself in another person, that I find validity in the other, which the other again obtains in me. This dialectic of love is the most enormous contradiction. Analytical understanding cannot solve this contradiction. Positive psychology, sociology, or futurology can describe and analyse the circumstances under which the dialectic of love does or does not enfold a particular culture, society, personality, behavioural organism or natural environment, but they cannot penetrate into its inner structure. This can be done only on the phenomenological level of dialectical reason. The dialectic of love is so impenetrable by analytic, instrumental reason, because there is nothing harder than this punctuality of the self-consciousness of the lovers to be which is negated in the dialectical process of love, but which the lovers should nevertheless have as something affirmative. The dialectic of love is at the same time the production as well as the dissolution of this contradiction. As this dissolution, the dialectic of love is the socio-ethical unity of marriage and family. It transforms the lovers into one person and constitutes their marital and finally familial solidarity.

INCLINATION AND DECISION

In the early stage of liberal capitalistic society for Hegel, marriage is essentially a socio-ethical form of communicative action. Hegel criticises particularly the natural law theories of traditional societies, since most of them considered marriage only in terms of its physical aspects, according to what it is by nature. Most natural lawyers in antiquity and the middle ages saw marriage only as a sexual relationship, and every entrance to its other determinations was blocked off. But for Hegel it is no less rude and barbarous for philosophers, theologians, and social scientists in modern society to understand marriage merely as a bourgeois contract, a concept which belongs in the much lower sphere of right and no longer in the higher familial dimension. According to Hegel's predecessor, the bourgeois enlightener Emmanuel Kant, in the marriage contract the mutual arbitrariness of the married individuals comes to an agreement concerning their own sexual functions. Marriage is degraded into the form of a contract between the marriage partners about the mutual use of their sexual organs. Likewise Hegel rejects a third theory prevalent in liberal capitalistic society, which makes marriage consist merely in love. Hegel objects to this idea since love, as feeling, allows for contingency in every respect, a form which social morality must not have. While in his own theory Hegel determines marriage as a socio-ethical love, he hopes by such definition to eliminate from marriage its transitory, capricious and merely subjective element, which according to the contemporary and bourgeois futurologist has become so prevalent in advanced capitalistic society.

Hegel differentiates between a subjective and objective starting point of marriage and family. The subjective starting point can be mainly either the particular inclination of the two persons who want to get married, or the provision and arrangement of the parents, relatives, the whole extended family, etc. The objective starting point of marriage and family is the free consent of the persons to become one person, to give up their natural and singular personality in the marital unity, which in this respect means a self-limitation, but which is in reality their liberation insofar as they gain in their marital and familial solidarity their substantial self-consciousness through the abandonment of their accidental self-consciousness. For Hegel, it is an objective socio-ethical determination, thereby a socio-moral right and duty for every man and woman to enter marriage. How the external starting point of the marriage is constituted, is by its nature contingent and depends particularly on the formation of reflection which has been reached by a certain society in the process of social evolution as the self-constitutive learning process of the human species. Here one extreme possibility is, that the arrangement of the well-meaning parents makes the beginning concerning the marital and familial life of their sons or daughters. The mutual inclination begins to grow in the two persons, who have been determined for the union of love by their parents, as soon as they are informed about the parental arrangement. The other extreme possibility is that the mutual inclination appears first in the infinitely particularised persons, who then make their own arrangements to get married with more or less parental consultation. For Hegel, the first possibility, or generally the way in which the decision for marriage makes the beginning and has the mutual inclination for its consequence, so that at the point of actual marriage both elements are united, is the better way in socio-ethical terms. In case of the second possibility, it is the infinitely particular peculiarity of the individual subject which makes valid its pretension. It is connected with the modern societies' principle of free subjectivity or subjective freedom. Hegel discovers that in modern dramas and other artistic presentations in which the love of the sexes constitutes the fundamental interest, an element of penetrating frostiness is carried into the heat of the presented sexual passion through the complete contingency connected with it as well as through the fixation of the whole interest on the sexuality of the lovers, which may be of infinite interest for them but not as such. To be sure, the element of coldness in sexual love as portrayed by modern art since Hegel—e.g., in the novels of Flaubert or the dramas of Strindberg and their followers—is not the reflection of the Christian but rather of the bourgeois principle of subjective freedom. According to Hegel, in patriarchal primitive and traditional societies in which the female sex is held in low esteem, the parents dispose over the marriage of their daughters in terms of their own arbitrariness without asking the individuals. The girls put up with this arrangement, since the particularity of their feeling doesn't make any pretension yet at the archaic or traditional stage of evolution. The girl wants merely *a* man, not *this* man, and the man is merely concerned with *a* woman as such and not with *this* woman. Under other circumstances in archaic and traditional society, considerations of property, business connections and political purposes can be determinant factors. Where marriage is instrumentalised for purposes alien to its nature in this way, great undue hardships can occur. Contrary to this, in modern liberal capitalistic society the subjective starting point of marriage and family—the falling in love—is considered to be the only important one. People have the idea that every man and woman must wait until his or her hour has come, and one individual can give his or her love only to this particular person of the other sex. In the last analysis, Hegel is as critical of the archaic and traditional way to get married, based on parental decision in which the universal triumphs over the particular, as of the modern way, grounded in personal inclination of those to be married, in which the subject dominates and soon destroys the substance. Following Hegel's dialectical developmental logic beyond the boundaries of modern society, we may anticipate in a post-capitalistic, post-modern, reconciled society a form of marriage and family in which neither the universal would overwhelm the particular nor the subject the substance, but in which for the first time in man's evolution particular and universal, subject and substance, inclination and decision, self-actualisation and unity, pleasure and duty, satisfaction and obligation, joy and dignity, freedom and solidarity, eros and logos would be mediated through each other and balanced with each other.

CRITIQUE OF BOURGEOIS MARRIAGE AND FAMILY

At a later stage of liberal capitalistic society, Marx criticises Hegel's concept as well as the whole bourgeois theory and practice of marriage and family and out of this critique develops his own view.[10] According to Marx, from the very beginning of their historical development as a species, men and women, who make their own life daily new through work, begin to produce other humans, to propagate themselves. Through it arises the relationship between man and woman, parents and children, the family. This family is in the beginning of man's social evolution the only social relationship. In the further development of the human species, when the multiplication of needs produces new social relations and the increase of the population creates new needs, the family becomes a subordinate social unit. As one of many subsystems in liberal capitalistic society, the family must be treated and developed in terms of the existing empirical data, not according to the notion of the family. While Hegel penetrates through the facts into the dialectical deep structure of the family, Marx recommends a notionless empirical study of marriage and family. On an empirical basis, Marx defends the contemporary communistic movement against the bourgeois charge that it intends to liquidate the family. Marx launches an empirical critique of the situation of the family in liberal capitalistic society. In Marx's view, the present bourgeois family is based on capital, on private acquisition. What for Hegel was only the negative external moment in the process of the family—dead property—Marx discovers to be its very essence. According to Marx, the family exists in its completely developed form only for the bourgeoisie. But the bourgeois family finds its complement in the forced celibacy of the proletarians and in public prostitution. Marx predicts that the family of the bourgeois will cease to exist with the abolition of this its complement and both will disappear with the disappearance of capital. While Marx does indeed foresee the withering away of bourgeois marriage and family with the decline of the antagonistic capitalistic society, he thereby in no way precludes the reconstruction of the family as a new marital and familial community in the framework of a post-capitalistic, post-modern reconciled society, in which neither men nor women nor children will be instrumentalised or commodified, but will be free in solidarity.

NEW MARITAL AND FAMILIAL COMMUNITY

In advanced capitalistic society, the Marxist Horkheimer observes, like Marx before him, that the difference of the existence of social groups, conditioned through the type of income, has effects upon the structure of the family.[11] Horkheimer admits that particularly in times of relatively bearable conditions on the labour market, a large number of proletarian families is formed in accordance with the pattern of the bourgeois family. Horkheimer knows that particularly under early capitalism, the family authority takes horrible forms in consequence of the compulsion to let children work. But in spite of all this, so Horkheimer argues, there is in these proletarian families nevertheless present the potential for other relationships, for a new community. It is true, the law of big industry does destroy the snug home. It drives often not only the husband, but also the wife into a hard existence outside the home. One can no longer speak of the satisfying autonomous value of the private existence. In the extreme case, the family constitutes the reachable form of sexual satisfaction and beyond that, the multiplication of cares and sorrows. But on this basis, so Horkheimer observes, where the original interest in the family has disappeared to a large extent, the same feeling of solidarity can arise in the family which binds proletarians together outside the familial dimension. According to Horkheimer, in organised capitalistic society the utopia is present of a future society without poverty and injustice. With this idea is connected the effort to make things better and to bring about a reconciled society. This effort characterises, instead of the bourgeois individualistic motives, the relationships in the proletarian family in which a new solidarity is arising. According to Horkheimer, out of the sufferings from liberal and advanced capitalistic society, which oppresses human existence under the sign of bourgeois authority, a new community of husband and wife and of children can come into existence. This new marital and familial community will certainly not be closed up in the old bourgeois mode against other families of the same type or against individuals of one's own group. The children are not educated as future heirs. They are therefore also no longer experienced by their parents in the specific bourgeois sense as their own. Insofar as the work for the children does not only concern the daily livelihood, it goes over into the fulfilment of the historical task to create a reconciled society in which they and others can live a more humane life. The education upon which this new sentiment of familial solidarity radiates, teaches the children—less maybe through conscious instruction than through involuntary expression of voice and bearing—to differentiate very clearly between the knowledge of facts and their recognition. Horkheimer is sober enough to see, that with the development of unemployment in organised, capitalistic society—which makes free labour not only insecure but finally also into a privilege for relatively limited and carefully selected groups of the population—this type of a future orientated family will, of course, become scarce. The complete demoralisation and the absolute hopelessness which arises from the submission under every master have their effects in the family. Powerlessness and the lack of opportunity for productive work have already dissolved the beginnings of a new type of education to a large extent in organised capitalistic society. For Horkheimer, the fact that the exchange principle of bourgeois society has penetrated the family, appears as disintegration. The critical theorist finds the fact affirmed that even in the family in case of exchange, the economically stronger one is always right. Who is better qualified is the victor. The whole psychoanalysis of marriage difficulties rests upon the acknowledgment of the criterium of exchange. According to this criterium, it is not healthy that the one gives more than the other. Precisely, therefore, the one is over-reached who does not bring with him or her more than love. The extension of the principle of exchange must break up the family. According to Horkheimer, the power of the father as feudal lord, which has asserted itself in the hiding place of the household even into organised capitalistic society has rightly been replaced by the higher principle of exchange among free people. But the real freedom is not yet realised. Until freedom will really exist and the old traditional forms have really been overcome, only the exuberance in the individual life can leave the principle of exchange behind. Horkheimer predicts that the principle of exchange will continue to vegetate on in different countries, when the world has long been overrun by the barbarians who today determine the social development. Horkheimer thinks of the positivists of all shades who, in West and East, prepare if not Future II—the thermonuclear holocaust, then at least Future I—the totally administered technocratic and bureaucratic society. According to Horkheimer in the now disintegrating institution of the bourgeois marriage and family, the man earned the living and the woman took care of the household. The man had value as the breadwinner, therefore as lord and master, the woman as *passivum*, as object. She had to be supported. How deeply wrong this judgement was comes now to the foreground, since now at last through the change of the woman's function, civilisation has lost substance. The woman's infinitely shaded, mostly subtle and at the same time more exhausting work than that of the husband is automated like that of the latter. The rest appears as mere drudge. The woman has equal rights. The distorted, mendacious stereotype of the expensive wife and the bad mother-in-law is fundamentally only an unconscious consolation for the lost possibility of happiness which marriage and family sometimes contained. The woman of the past is gone—as is romantic love. Instrumental reason has taken their place. With the disappearance of the 'Care of the Housewife', the men become colder, and the women imitate them.

When Horkheimer reflects back on his own marriage, he must say that many beautiful aspects of it rested on what he calls the moral quality of action, which again is not possible without theology.[12] It consists simply in the fact that my own life, even if I must sacrifice it for the other human being, is beautified by the reactions of the other. Horkheimer's marriage through the years took such a form, that his late wife not only would have sacrificed her life for him, but that she became for him the highest. This experience is the reason why Horkheimer thought so critically about the dissolution of erotic love in advanced capitalistic society, which on the other hand he considered to be necessary. Three years before his death in 1973, to the great astonishment of many of his students and friends, Horkheimer tried to justify Pope Paul VI's encyclical letter, *Humanae Vitae*, which forbids Catholics to use artificial means of birth control. The Pope in writing the encyclical appeals to divinely instituted natural law, Horkheimer in defending it, to the critical theory of society. According to Horkheimer, the critical theory has a double task. It wants to signify what ought to be changed. But it must also name what is to be preserved. It has therefore also the task to show which price we must pay for this or that measure, for this or that progress. For 'the pill', so Horkheimer argues, we must pay with the death of erotic love. For Horkheimer, love has its foundation in longing for the beloved person. It is not free from sexuality. The greater the longing for union with the beloved human being, the greater is the love. If this taboo of sexuality is superseded and if the barrier falls which produces longing, then love loses its basis. According to Horkheimer, the pill transforms *Romeo and Juliet* into a museum piece. Horkheimer in no way denies that the pill is progress in relationship to the Third World, underdeveloped countries in Africa, Asia, and Latin America, in relation to the Damocles sword of overpopulation. But Horkheimer considered it to be his duty to make clear to people, that we must carry the costs for this progress and that the price consists in the acceleration of the loss of longing, finally the death of love. Horkheimer was certainly deeply horrified by the possibility and' probability of the arrival of Future I—the totally administered society or Future II—thermonuclear war. But he nevertheless lived and hoped for a new form of marriage and family, which would be characterised by the dialectic of love, by the balance of warm solidarity and personal liberation and which would constitute the anticipation and finally the very core of Future III—the reconciled society, in which the life of all men and women would be more beautiful, longer, better, freer from suffering and which would be more favourable for the enfolding of the spirit.

Notes

1. M. Porter *Critical Theory of the Family* (New York 1978), chap. 2, 6, 7.
G. W. F. Hegel *Grundlinien der Philosophie des Rechts* (Stuttgart 1964) pp. 237-262.
K. Marx *Die Frühschriften* (Stuttgart 1953) pp. 25-27, 111-112.
M. Horkheimer (ed.) *Studien uber Autoritat und Familie* (Paris 1936) pp. 3-76, 77-135, 136-228.
M. Horkheimer *Zur Kritik der instrumentellen Vernunft* (Frankfurt a.M. 1967) pp. 269-287, 288-301.
M. Horkheimer *Notizen 1950 bis 1969 und Dammerung* (Frankfurt a.M. 1974) pp. 59, 138, 203.
M. Horkheimer *Die Sehnsucht nach dem ganz Anderen* (Hamburg 1970) pp. 72-75.
2. R. Fernandez (ed.) *The Future as a Social Problem* (Santa Monica, Cal. 1977) p. 158.
3. M. Daly 'Feminism and the prospects for change' in Fernandez *The Future* pp. 89-101.
4. W. Goode 'World revolution and family patterns' in Fernandez *The Future* pp. 158-169.
5. E. Cornish etc. *The Study of the Future* (Washington D.C. 1977) p. 4.
6. R. E. Farson 'Why good marriages fail?' in Fernandez *The Future* pp. 169-176.
7. Cornish *The Study* pp. 27, 31-32, 49, 51.
8. Hegel *Grundlinien* pp. 182-183, 266-267.
G. W. F. Hegel *Enzyklopädie der philosophischen Wissenschaften im Grundriss* (Hamburg 1959) pp. 387-388.
9. Hegel *Grundlinien* pp. 237-239, 239-249, 249-251, 251-260, 261-262, 263.
10. Marx *Die Frühschriften* pp. 25-27, 111-112, 355, 543.
11. Horkheimer *Studien* pp. 71-73.
Horkheimer *Notizen* pp. 59, 138, 203.
Horkheimer *Zur Kritik* pp. 287, 300-301.
12. Horkheimer *Die Sehnsucht* pp. 73-74.

Jacques Grand'Maison

The Modern Family: Locus of Resistance or Agency of Change?

THE FIGURE I choose to represent my understanding of the situation of
the family at present is that of a basic electrical circuit in which a great
number of fuses have blown under the impact of the currents and back-
currents of cultural, socio-political and economico-political revolutions.

Accordingly, any explosion in the society as a whole would seem to give
rise to an implosion in the family. For the family has lost its rôle as a social
thermostat and has become a mere sounding-box. For example, an uncertain, chaotic society soon leads to temporary marriage, broken homes and
a fall in the birth-rate.

Therefore family structures no longer shape and serve as models for
society and its institutions. The reverse has been observable since the
advent of the modern city and modern industry. Some pundits draw from
this observation a doubtful and at best superficial conclusion: we should
mend or change the system as a whole before attending to the family.
Others are afraid of a retrograde conservative attitude on the part of
those who still see the family as a basic unit.

Some critics also sense the danger of Fascism, not forgetting how the
various bands of 'colonels' seized power in different countries on the
pretext of saving the 'family and the nation'.

These analyses are, however, a little too simplistic. For instance, are we
to overlook the often dramatic fate of the family unit in capitalist
countries and under totalitarian systems alike? And what about the new
contradictions and assurances which are beginning to bring other life-
styles and other social relations into married and family experience? This
tendency is growing, particularly among young couples of the rising
generations. One instance is the questioning of property relations

47

between husband and wife, and between parents and children. I shall return to this topic. I shall try first to give an account of the situation which I posed in terms of an electrical circuit.

A DEAD INSTITUTION?

Many of the social functions that accrued to the family have passed in part to other institutions. I would cite education, security, social status, leisure and a number of everyday occasions as to a considerable extent—so it seems—unconcerned with the family.

Married and family relations have been weakened. The divorce rate and the generation gap bear witness to this. Old people are dumped together. Adolescents come together outside the family. And the family has a short life lasting only as long as childhood. Even then, however, the husband-wife relationship appears uncertain, especially since the feminist revolt. But even before then women working outside the home had deeply changed internal and external family relations.

Geographical, vocational and social mobility, change of all kinds, and the upsets of urban life have seriously affected all the foundations of stabilisation and continuity in the family. There is also the major problem of accommodation in most cities.

The short-term society has also had a constantly corrosive effect on long-lasting relationships in the married and family universe. Transient fashions, obsolescent products, impulse buying with credit cards, tranquillisers of all kinds, the stimuli of advertising, and above all short-term relations in shops, at school, at work, in leisure pursuits and so on, may be cited in this respect. As a result the family adopts the same split and fragmented way of life. Getting married and having children are frightening long-term commitments. Better to enjoy the freedom that allows one to change one's partner, job, motor car or dwelling.

In this ephemeral instant-coffee age, groups are formed and disperse at an ever-quicker rate. This situation is rationalised by questioning not only lasting relationships but the very principle of institutionalisation. Marriage, for instance, would be in this perspective an occasion of boredom, routine and immobility, and at most a bourgeois contract on a scrap of paper. Like the State or the school it is marked down for extinction. The objection is no longer to the inadequacy of institutions or even to this or that inappropriate model, but to the necessity of institutions as means of organising collective life. This is an odd reversion to the primitive liberalism of the 'invisible hand' which brings so-called independent individuals together in society.

Capitalist economics and politics often do not take the individual into account, and mar the social relations of the working classes while concealing the influence of the ruling élites. In this way they make family life very difficult for very many citizens of capitalist societies. Some left-wingers who condemn the family and marriage are blind accomplices of this process. A system which sentences the family to be primarily a social unit of consumption shows its inhumanity all the more clearly.

Some criticisms have discerned the pitfalls of recent liberal pleas for the retention of the family. Historically, the family has often served to transmit and interiorise the social order desired by the dominant group. Faced with an increasing number of attacks, ruling élites take advantage of the traditional rôle of the family; they are once again taking an interest in the family as a power which allows the social reproduction of rich and poor, privileged and disadvantaged. To be sure, there is also the buffer zone of the middle classes which are often characterised by their interest in the family. The ruling classes find it strategically advantageous to ingratiate themselves with the middle classes in precisely this area.

The 'murder of the father' was translated initially into scientific and political revolutions before entering the spheres of education, work and the family. First, there was the rise of democracy and its overthrow of hierarchical structures. But that has proved an imcomplete victory if we consider the preponderance of autocratic régimes in the world, whether they are military, financial or totalitarian. In the West the revolution of 'horizontal relations' is affecting all institutions and more especially the family. After young people, women have begun to challenge paternal and male authority.

But the cultural revolution goes even further—like son, like father, like daughter, like mother, as it were. It is all as if the revolution in question had emphasised the great American myth of golden adolescence. Many adults adopt the ways of the young. Admittedly one might say that these ways themselves owe a lot to some adult influences from the arts and the mass media, and from advertising and salesmen. But it seems impossible to refute the importance of the 'youth' phenomenon. This hitherto unknown social laboratory is neither an isolated sub-system nor a unique sub-culture. For instance, the relaxed attitude of many young people to work can make their elders uneasy about their own attitude to the value of work in their lives. And then there is the problem of freedom. . . . Yet this contrary influence carries with it extreme tensions that too often prove unbearable for a modern psyche in so buffeted and fragile a state.

An unsure and explosive society, a blocked or at least very uncertain future, a major sensation of being on the edge of a universal crisis, the admitted impotence of experts and leaders before major domestic and world problems, an internal disestablishment of major institutions—these are phenomena which are at least sensed by a great number of people and have a considerable effect on family life and central family decisions. How are people to decide appropriately about their children and the future in a society that seems to have none, and in a social situation apparently without any discernible outcome? How can people effectively look forward to an extended process of education when to all intents and purposes it is a mere drop of water in an ocean of uncontrollable influences?

AN UNEXPECTED FINDING

The family, then, has seemed to be in its death throes. All the attacks I have cited above would be enough to make its fuses blow. Yet the family has not disappeared more or less swiftly as some English sociologists predicted just before the Second World War. Admittedly, the uncertainties, disappointments, inadequacies and rejections seem to increase. But at the same time there is an unexpected revaluation of the family. In spite of the ambiguities, there are positive features in this revival (I shall not, however, pause here to discuss family models, for in the present perspective it is more exact to say that *certain types of family* are disappearing whereas others are coming into existence. The same is true of the cultural rôles which partly determine substructural functions).

For some time parents have had recourse to experts for definitions of their educational rôle. Mother had the latest work of Dr Spock to hand. The problem-child was entrusted to an institution. In disadvantaged environments the school was offered as a substitute for inadequate families. The State financed foster-families for children of 'irresponsible parents'. And so we come back to the primary, natural core of the family, and observe a revaluation of it as an essential environment.

In the fragmented, paradoxically programmed city, the family remains one of the few loci of total integration of the human individual. The specialisation and parallelism of institutions tend to dissolve experience. A considerable number of the inhabitants of our urban world look for a place or for places where they can be wholly themselves. They want somewhere where they can talk about their work, their love-affairs, their leisure activities, politics, and so on. They are in search of a multi-dimensional solidarity, one might say. And the family seems to be precisely one of those few centres of integration. Of course that is far from being always the case; yet the other, similar places of resort are too yielding to have any integrational effect, as is the case, for instance, with 'mutual support' or 'caring' groups without the permanency associated with the family.

Relieved of a number of burdensome functions, the modern family is becoming a kind of extremely valuable socio-affective centre. It persists more by virtue of the quality of its relationships than by any functional necessity. In this sense family experience enjoys an unprecedented air of freedom. Its internal relations become all the richer because of the variety of ways in which it is open to the external world; at the same time those relations afford a unique kind of experience that is otherwise often unobtainable in present-day society. In this way many people are rethinking the breaks and unthinking rejections of the past that were closed to any possibility of a redefinition of the family. There was in the past too great an adherence to a traditional model quite out of phase with new patterns of life. This barrier had to be removed. Yet as a mere reaction this did not lead to new investigations of any positive value.

The growing importance attributed to private life is realised in a new intensity of family life. The weekdays have a dispersive effect but the weekend brings people together. During the week, the individual is, as it were, forced in on himself and conviviality is at a low ebb; people come to and go from the home at various times. Peter gets back from the technical college at two o'clock, whereas Mary returns from school at four, and mother is back just in time to get a meal ready. Father has to stay late at the office and his supper has to be kept hot for him. Whether at school, work or elsewhere, the much-praised flexibility of a multitude of time-tables paradoxically makes it all the more impossible to pursue consistent social relationships and joint ventures. All this is a challenge to family life. But nowadays people are beginning to react to this process. Many families are determined to have the weekend and privileged moments of privacy and communal life for themselves. In some families even television has lost some of its power of attraction. People are beginning to experience more of the joy of mutual rediscovery and communication within the family.

But in the long run this kind of fragmented everyday existence with all its discontinuity is not compensated for by the possibility of valuable new experience. People want something less nervous and more permanent. Something tougher in fact. At one time the kernel of life was hidden under far too unyielding a shell of family structures and moral rules. Now that people have discovered the kernel, they are without the shell that not only stopped it from rotting but allowed it a chance of renewal. The displacement of the family has brought with it the loss of, as it were, a human economy of life. A traditional wisdom, with all the benefits of descent and generational links, has gone too. Some have condemned these cultural transmissions as if they bore with them only dead, useless or obsolete things. Nowadays, however, people find they do not have the roots they need in order to communicate with the riches of the past. Are we courageous enough to acknowledge the real causes of this crisis of 'transmission' in our western societies? Sophisticated social techniques and omnipresent communications media have not resolved the complex problem of cultural transmission, and it is questionable whether they could do so. In this respect, too, there is a reversion to family experience in the form of an attempt to redefine it in terms of new values that I shall try to outline.

History teaches us that in difficult times family bonds tighten up. This is observable in wartime, for instance. Many people feel that the easy prosperity of yesteryear has gone for ever. Even the secure feel threatened. Abundance tends to disperse people, whereas penury brings them together. Furthermore, the interplay of social classes has changed, especially when the mass of the 'unclassed' is growing. I shall not touch here on the political aspects of the problem, which I have examined elsewhere. I want primarily to emphasise the anthropological phenomenon of deep bonds which are forged in the course of shared trials, alongside or at the heart of conflicts which are no less profound. I suspect that the present revival of the family owes a lot to this widespread feeling that life will soon get very much worse. But I am not unaware of the danger of having recourse to the family as a mere place for withdrawal, a conservative fortress.

INITIAL CRITICISMS

My initial remarks are purely descriptive. Both heights and declivities reveal a degree of bewilderment evoked to a large extent by the major fears of our age. There is a collective fear of chaos and an individual fear of death, remarked respectively by sociologists and psychiatrists. But we must not allow these fears to prevent our attempt at understanding, or to obscure the reality. There is also a danger that the urgent need to see the situation more clearly could lead to a naïve search for a happy theory that would explain everything—the common denominator of all change, the one true solution.

We must remember the multitude of currents and back-currents I have already referred to: the fragmented plurality of cultural changes in the psycho-social, economic and political realms. Within and without the family there is no logical set of factors to be found which would allow one to offer the right system or ideal structure. To endow reality with a coherence it does not possess is to adopt an attitude which comprises though it obscures both fear and flight, and sometimes even a will to manipulation or domination. Hence we shall leave to one side the tedious problems, the even deeper riches and as yet unexplored possibilities.

I shall concentrate instead on the examples of a far from orthodox hypothesis which might perhaps refute the apparent evidence of accepted analyses.

THE HEIGHTS AND DEPTHS OF THE NUCLEAR FAMILY

The western family had gradually become limited to a nucleus of three or four members: the father, mother and one or two children.

This nucleus seems to me explosive because of its extremely high emotional concentration. It all seems to be an extreme demonstration of the Oedipus theory. In this constricted atmosphere, the child does not enjoy the same chances of alternatives and compensation, such as might accrue from more diversified lateral relations, with, for instance an uncle or a grandmother, with a close and attentive teacher. What is in question is, of course, contacts with other adults, somewhat as in the extended family of the past. Nowadays, the swift extension of the educational system has led to the employment of an enormous number of young schoolteachers. The added work-specialisation and a form of organisation close to anonymity make it even more difficult for young people to establish qualitative and personal relationships with true adults. I suspect that many contemporary problems are linked to these structural changes and the attendant lack of adult and communitarian mediation.

In a restricted family nucleus which comprises all the members' intense affective relationships, the Oedipal drama becomes difficult to control if one member or another of the family displays pathological symptoms. Even if that kind of defect is not apparent, the exclusive proximity makes the family claustrophobic. It is often remarked that some instances of dissatisfaction or even rebellion among young people arise from the distance or inadequate presence of the parents. In many instances, however, the opposite is true. Breaks are caused by the claustrophobic pressures of a too restrictive circle where there is hardly any possibility of emotional distance or compensatory relationships. The affective registers of age and generations are too limited. The paradox is that the parents are too close, exclusive, 'caring', and ubiquitous emotionally. This can happen even when a mother works outside the home and the father is hardly ever there. The emotional process occurs at another level. I shall try to delineate it more exactly.

In former societies, there was no awareness of what Freud and other pundits have discerned in this respect. Yet there was an understanding of the need to enlarge the affective circle, and to allow other identifications, and other psychological and social relationships, not only through the extended family but by means of all kinds of communitarian mediations. It is not necessary to include among these possibilities forms of education tending to allow emotional and social diversification. For example, there was the long time spent by an apprentice with his master, or by a future warrior who went to another family to learn the way to knighthood. The notion of preceptors or spiritual directors had a similar intention.

Recently, even, a young person was able to attain to a certain degree of identification with some teachers throughout his years in school and college, and so on. There was a traditional wisdom behind all this.

Today, the disappearance of real intermediary environments and communities often delivers up the individual to his own subject self within an anonymous social organisation. Even the narrow circle of the nuclear family increases this affective isolation without any worthwhile communitarian support. The organisation of day nurseries in their present form only accentuates the problems. I think that we need a new strategy for resocialisation that would allow a more intelligently developmental form of emotional and social communication, with much more clearly defined and articulated stages. This strategy would not be afforded solely by techniques and structures which tend to a mechanical construction of standardised human relations.

I shall return to this important problem in the present development of the family and other common social loci. I merely wanted to show in my hypothesis how sometimes it is necessary to escape from received situations in order to get round some dead-ends of present family analysis. There is not necessarily any question of 'reinventing' the extended family or of restoring a former family model. To demystify a form of pseudo-progress, to take advice from some examples of traditional wisdom, and to show the non-congruence of accepted or fashionable diagnoses, is not to condemn one's own times, but rather to free critical thought and creative action for rich historical and possible new experiences. The past has known many different and complex family models; others are possible or in process of formation today.

The nuclear family has known its summits of achievement. Its recent development, affected as it is by the impoverishment of social relations in the techno-bureaucratic society, would seem to lead to dead-ends and calls for far-reaching renewal. We have to take the whole complex of social relations into account. But I think that a wrong way to do that would be to resort to a form of globalism which speedily disqualifies the efforts that might be made in the associated schools, families, working environment, and locality, merely in order to anticipate on a small scale what is to be attained on a large scale by means of major essential collective instruments—such as a political party or a trade union. If we neglect these humble everyday forms of mediation, we become unwitting accomplices of the lies of publicity, and of meaningless collective experiences, such as the ubiquitous commercialised forms of leisure activity—accomplices, too, of many numbing and alienating deviations. For instance, a sexual revolution might well be legitimate, but be rendered deviant by the pornography industry. And can we really talk of the benefits of a revolution in electronic communications that places a nation

in front of the television set? What about the spiritual renewal supposed
to emerge from the East or far-distant stars which suffers from an obsession with 'evil spirits' or the threat of extra-terrestrial visitors? All such
changes stop people from really knowing how to lead their lives in
themselves, and roundabout them, as lives which give a meaning to
everything else and make them a real contribution to the great human
venture.

THE FAMILY IS STILL A LOCUS OF SOCIAL TRUTH

The very restriction of the family reveals certain features of modern life
which are often indiscernible on the macrocosmic scale. For instance, the
individual freed from the rule of habits and customs which had become
almost deterministic or dogmatic, is still hesitant when faced with the
possibilities of his own freedom. Perhaps this partly explains the con-
formisms and alienations cited in the foregoing, and all the inexperience,
non-adaptation and fear of choice and even increased powers. These
factors are to some extent contributory. A number of people do hesitate
at the thought of greater individual responsibility, at marriage, at the idea
of the child they are going to have, at most lasting vocational, social and
other commitments. For very many people, opposition or resistance to
change is more or less consciously associated with a refusal to choose, to
flight from the novel demands of freedom.

The paradoxes grow in number particularly in the family. The more
people resort to the family as one of the last centres of permanence, the
more they look on it as the scapegoat for all incomprehensible or uncontrollable constraints. There is hardly ever any awareness of the absence of
a social matrix for the individual as well as for the family. The latter
becomes the privileged locus of dissatisfaction and challenge. The uncertainty of social relations becomes a questioning of family and marital
relations. It is no great distance from the short-term relations of the city to
rationalisations about divorce which is no longer seen as an exceptional
setback. Very few people see the social sub-structure of the moral question.

Man and the modern city suffer from 'chronopathy' (an inability to
locate oneself in chronological time). There are no longer any appropriately rhythmic and circumscribed social times and locations. The hope
of love and the extended possibilities of the family suffer all the more
because of that. Hence the ambiguity of the revival of the family, which
sometimes manifests itself as the search for an artificial hothouse, a
replacement matrix, and a compensatory form of permanence. Some
people revert to former models without seeing them in terms of modern

urban life and their own cultural development. Their plaint is very revealing: 'We have traduced our heritage . . . we have made superficial changes while forgetting what is essential and here we are without tradition, experience or recourse for the future'. The essential component of such talk is the accepted model, and history is defined solely in terms of the past. But truly human time (from the western viewpoint of history as something to be made) is overlooked. Of course the instantaneous nature of urban life leads to such short-circuits. No advance has been made in either regard.

My previous question has to be asked again: Do we first have to define social life as a whole? But where are we to begin? The global ideological approach of critical minorities makes very slow progress. It meets with enormous obstacles both at the base and at the summit of social, economic and political organisation. It seems utopian and abstract. It appears to demand the sacrifice of present freedoms and to have to pass through the totalitarian melting-pot at the almost inevitable risk of staying there. The rising generations are too anxious to live freely to take any serious part in this collectivist mêlée. After a more or less libertarian and anarchic period, new movements are observable in schools and colleges, in work-places, in living accommodation, and in love.

A NEW POLITICAL DIRECTION

The fact that some people reject both in marriage and in the family any possessive form of relationship (between man and woman, between parents and children) is a possible challenge to a society constructed primarily on property, which establishes a reified, monetary form of relationship whereas solidarity directly connotes a human relationship.

At the heart of the experience of love, young couples are attempting possible new forms—different forms of individuality and social being, emotional and cultural relations, a more human division of labour, time and place. Perhaps they are more aware of what kind of city they want, what commodities to produce or consume. Their method is more 'political' and more 'economic' than it seems at first. Perhaps their wager is more valid than that of the moraliser or that of the ideologues of the new dreamed-of system which is relegated to an unknown tomorrow.

There is, then, a certain grassroots revolution which co-exists with a too abstract, cold and mechanical political revolution that is also extremely naïve in its loyalty to the promise of new structures, as if they would automatically offer happiness, virtue and justice.

A very revealing test is possible in this area. What sort of love relationship, matrimonial relationship, parenthood and everyday solidarity are actually lived by the militant radicals or the champions of the social order said to be in need of revival? It is on that level that we can verify the human element or the inhumanity of a political militant. The same is true of power as of possession when it becomes an absolute end. The demands of an authentic marital or family relationship call in question most present-day ideological projects.

The most radical family ventures challenge society in various, very actual ways. There is the urgent question of housing and all the associated problems (transport, working conditions, nurseries, and so on). Family life challenges the appropriateness of global and local changes in regard to basic everyday relationships. One need only mention in this respect the far-reaching educational crisis, and certain administrative, vocational and even trade-union practices from which children suffer, to realise this. The actual fate of children is a challenge to all the large and small solutions propounded by society, its experts and its radical ideologues.

Whether the child, the aged or the working man is in question, we are always faced with the same absolute situation of the human being stripped of everything but his human condition to put at stake. Whatever régime is in power, a society is always to be judged primarily in terms of the fate that it accords the bare human being, unaccommodated man. I hold this conviction not only on the basis of the Gospel but on that of family experience, which demands such an absolute postulation of the question. So-called liberal, progressive solutions 'for adults' are often silent as to their effects on children. One is only five, ten or twenty years old once in one's life. There is also the fact that there are few alternatives for the child (see, for instance, Truffaut's film *Argent de Poche—Pocket Money*).

Our public debates remain very superficial. They are able to spend a long time on the questions of a greater liberalisation of divorce or abortion without asking any serious questions about the necessary conditions for building a solid, lasting and qualitatively good marriage and family. What the mass of ordinary people want is not above all the possibility of divorce, but that of the ability to set up a real family. Petty-bourgeois problems do the opposite. How hyprocritical that is. It is true, too, that a certain left-wing tendency leads to the same thing. They are both unaware of the actual, 'objective' situation of two fundamental classes—the integrated and the excluded.

Of course the family situation can be paradoxical. The family can in fact take up several social and cultural forms—egalitarian or authoritarian, open or closed, free or constrictive. It can be a centre of withdrawal, reaction and egotism. But we must not forget that historically the family has played hardly negligible rôles in opposition and liberation, for instance, to totalitarian powers, and also anticipatory rôles when confronted with new cultural and social demands. Contemporary experience offers much evidence that this is the case.

In sum, I am persuaded that in the techno-bureaucratic city of most present-day forms of government the family remains one of the few warm currents of humanity. If we allow this fundamental social material to decay, soon neither reform, nor revolution, nor the *status quo* will be possible, because the most basic human element will be absent.

Translated by John Cumming

PART II

Theological Response: The Quest for Intimacy

Roland E. Murphy

A Biblical Model of Human Intimacy:
The Song of Songs

THE COMPLEXITY of human intimacy is expressed in a series of
questions which Henri Nouwen presents in a volume entitled *Intimacy*:
'How can I find a creative and fulfilling intimacy in my relationship with
God and my fellowmen? How can a man be intimate with a woman, and
how a man with a man? What does intimacy mean in the life of a celibate
priest or in the community of religious? How can I be intimate with God
during the moments of celebration or silent prayer?'[1]

The Bible sheds some light on all these questions. Nowhere is 'intimacy' analysed as such. One is simply confronted with intimacy as expressed among humans, and between humans and God. Thus one can
single out the powerful expression of union and presence as expressed in
Ps. 139:

> Even before a word is on my tongue,
>   behold, O Lord, you know the whole of it.
> Behind me and before, you hem me in
>   and rest your hand on me . . .
> Truly you have formed my inmost being;
>   you knit me in my mother's womb (vv. 5-6, 13).

Or in the New Testament, the union between the vine and the branches
(John 15) and the Pauline doctrine of the Body of Christ (1 Cor. 12) can
be counted among Christian insights into intimacy. All these texts illus-
trate intimacy between the divine and the human. At the same time the
paradoxical nature of this relationship should be remembered. For the
Lord is never closer than when he is distant, as is expressed in the book of

Job, or by the author of Ps. 130 ('De Profundis') and as exemplified in the suffering and death of Christ.

In this essay we shall restrict our investigation to intimacy between the sexes as this is found in the Song of Songs. Although the ancient Near Eastern culture did not encourage an open display of affection, and even treated wives as the property of husbands, several expressions of intimacy are to be found in the Bible. Jacob's seven years of labour for Rachel are described as 'but a few days, because of the love he had for her' (Gen. 29:20). Amnon's love/hate relationship with his sister Tamar is recorded in 2 Sam. 13:13: 'the hatred with which he hated her was greater than the love with which he had loved her.'

It is particularly within the wisdom literature that human intimacy is featured. Friendship is a common topic in Proverbs and in Ecclesiasticus: 'He who is a friend is always a friend' (Prov. 17:17); 'a faithful friend is beyond price; he who finds one finds a treasure' (Sir. 6:15). Friends of course are to be tested, and not every relationship turned out to be beneficial. The sages were particularly concerned with the sexual relationship of man and woman, and the warnings delivered to young men are far more frequent than one has reason to expect (Prov. 6:24-7:27). But one must also keep in mind the attraction that the fertility rites of Canaan exercised upon the Israelites.

A good wife was prized beyond all else, a 'favour from the Lord' (Prov. 18:22; 31:11-31). But it must be admitted that the judgments are largely from the male point of view. This may be due to the style and values of an education which was primarily orientated to young men. In Prov. 5:18 the sage admonishes the young man: 'Have joy of the wife of your youth, your lovely hind, your graceful doe.' This language is reminiscent of the Song of Songs, which deservedly occupies a primary place in any discussion of human intimacy.

SONG OF SONGS

Modern biblical scholarship is almost unanimous in understanding the Song of Songs as referring to human sexual love. The ancient tradition of both Synagogue and Church referred it to the love of Yahweh/Christ for His People/Church. We will return to this view later, but for the present let us explore the Song as a witness to love between the sexes.

It makes no difference for our purposes, whether one regards the work as a unit or as a composition of disparate love songs. In its present form the Song describes the feelings of love between a man and a woman, and the interplay of these feelings is presented in a dialogue. The very beginning plunges one *in medias res*: 'Let him kiss me with the kisses of his mouth', says the woman. In the dialogue she addresses the Daughters of Jerusalem several times, but these seem merely to afford the woman an opportunity to speak more about her lover. They do not figure seriously in the development of the dialogue.

Presence/Absence

One of the key themes in the Song is the presence and/or absence of the lovers to each other. The fact of physical presence is, of course, important and obvious in that they speak to each other and cling to each other ('His left hand is under my head, and his right arm embraces me' 2:6; 8:3). But even more significant is absence, for it is the experience of absence which gives expression to the meaning of presence. It is not merely that the woman desires to arrange a rendezvous with the man ('Tell me, you whom my heart loves, where you pasture your flock . . .' 1:7). More frequently she is expressing her yearning for her lover who is absent:

> In my bed at night I sought him
>> whom my heart loves—
> I sought him but did not find him . . .
>> Have you seen him whom my heart loves?   (3:1-3).

> I opened to my lover—
>> but my lover had departed, gone
> I sought him but I did not find him;
>> I called to him but he did not answer me   (5:6).

These passages are doublets; both describe the same or similar nocturnal experiences (dream?) in which the woman feels the agony of the man's absence. Her determined search for him succeeds easily in ch. 3, and in ch. 6 it is woven into a dialogue with the Daughters of Jerusalem, which enables the woman to give a description of her lover (5:9-16) before she affirms that he was never really lost since he belongs to her (6:1-3).

Mutuality

Mutuality means the reciprocity of feelings between the lover and beloved. This is evidenced in many expressions, such as the garden motif:

> You are enclosed garden, my sister, my bride,
>> an enclosed garden, a fountain sealed.
> You are a park that puts forth pomegranates,
>> with all choice fruits   (4:12-13).

To this she replies:

> Let my lover come to his garden
>> and eat its choice fruits   (4:16b).

And he accepts her invitation:

> I have come to my garden, my sister, my bride;
>   I gather my myrrh and my spices   (5:1a).

When he describes her mouth 'like an excellent wine', she interrupts in order to say that it 'flows smoothly for my lover, spreading over the lips and the teeth (7:10). The 'sexual yearning' (*tᵉšûqāh*) that is used of the woman in Gen. 3:16 is now used of the man:

> I belong to my lover
>   and for me he yearns.

When he praises her as 'a lily among thorns', she replies that among men he is 'as an apple tree among the trees of the woods' (4:3).

Sensuousness

The role of the senses—seeing, hearing, touching—in the encounter of the man and woman is paramount:

> O my dove in the clefts of the rock,
>   in the secret recesses of the cliff,
> Let me see you,
>   let me hear your voice   (2:12).

He must ask her (but hardly seriously) to turn her eyes from him because of the torment they cause (6:5). In the 'embrace' refrain (2:6; 8:3) she describes herself in his arms, and she expresses the wish to be his sister in order that she might display her affection publicly (8:1). He proclaims that her lips drip honey, that sweetmeats and milk are under her tongue (4:11). He likens her to a palm tree that he will climb in order to take hold of the branches and fruit (7:9). She describes his scent as a sachet of myrrh that rests in her bosom, a cluster of henna (1:13-14), while for him the fragrance of her garments is 'the fragrance of Lebanon' (4:11), and she is the park that contains 'myrrh and aloes with all the finest spices' (4:14).

Throughout the Song there is a profusion of fruits and flowers: cedars and cypresses, lilies and thorns, nard and saffron, calamus and cinnamon, herbs and mandrakes, palms and nut garden. All sorts of animals appear: lions and leopards, gazelles and hinds, stag and fawn, sheep and ewes. This small work provides lively display of imaginative language that never ceases to surprise the reader, while it expresses the lyrical quality of sensuous love.

A 'theology' of love

It has often been remarked that as in the Book of Esther, the name of God is conspicuously absent in the Song of Songs. Perhaps there is a reference to the Lord in 8:6, where *šalhebetyāh* may indicate 'the flames of Yah (weh)'. Nevertheless, if there is no explicit mention of God, there is a profound and ultimately religious characterisation of love in 8:6,

> For stern as death is love,
>   relentless as the nether world is devotion.

How can Love be compared to Death? The point of the comparison is the power of death. That idea was very much part of the Israelite world view, and it derived from myth and experience (from which myth may be said to arise). The ancient Ugaritic poems describe for us the battle which Baal wages against Mot, the god of death. This theological warfare reflected the reality of human experience. In daily existence every living thing is pitted against death. This is so, not merely in the sense that death is the eventual enemy one must confront. But to the extent that one experiences non-life in the adversities and trials of daily existence—to that extent one is truly dead. Hence it is no exaggeration for the psalmist to hail the Lord as one who rescued him from death (Ps. 30:4). Death, then, is the irresistible power which pursues every human being. Love is compared to Death because it, too, pursues its object with intensity and will not cease until it grasps the beloved.

Divine Intimacy

The above sketch indicates how profoundly human is the description of love in the Song of Songs. I also indicated that the ancient tradition of both the Synagogue and the Church deserved to be treated.[2] How is one to understand the Song in terms of human *and* divine love?

It is we moderns who have difficulty with this question. But the Bible suggests that these loves are united and are not to be separated. Israel, it is true, understood that Yahweh was beyond sex; he had no consort, and the fertility rites were not the proper mode of worship for him. Yet the union between man and woman became a primary symbol for the expression of the relationship of the Lord to His People. The covenant between God and His People is consistently portrayed as a marriage. Hosea's own tragic marital experience seems to have suggested the full dimensions of Israel's relationship to the Lord:

> I will espouse you to me forever;
>   I will espouse you in right and in justice, in love and in mercy;
> I will espouse you in fidelity,
>   and you shall know the Lord   (Hos. 2:21-22).

This theme is developed by many of the prophets, and there is the bold image in Isaiah 62:4-5:

No more shall men call you 'Forsaken',
  or your land 'Desolate',
But you shall be called 'My Delight',
  and your land 'Espoused'.
For the Lord delights in you,
  and makes your land his spouse.
As a young man marries a virgin,
  your Builder shall marry you;
And as a bridegroom rejoices in his bride,
  so shall your God rejoice in you.

We are faced with the *fact* that Israel and later the Church interpreted the intimate language of the Song of Songs as portraying the love of God for His People. True, the traditional interpretation almost snuffed out what the Song has to say about human love. There were several incidental historical factors that supported this myopic tendency, such as the limited views of the community concerning sexual expression. But the insight of Synagogue and Church remains, and it suggests that we should ponder the relationship between divine love and human sexual love. If 'love is of God', and 'God is love' (1 John 4:7-8), the Song of Songs intimates that human love is a participation in divine love. Human intimacy derives its reality and validity because of God, because of his love. The love that human beings share is a participation in something divine. Can the community of faith appropriate this biblical insight?

Notes

1. Henri Nouwen *Intimacy* (Notre Dame 1969) p. 1.
2. See R. E. Murphy 'Towards a commentary on the Song of Songs' *Catholic Biblical Quarterly* 39 (1977) pp. 482-496.

John Kilgallen

Intimacy and the New Testament

'INTIMACY' can describe two situations. First, it can indicate nearness
or proximity, and simply that. Secondly, it can refer to a situation of
affection, candour, love. This distinction shows that not all relationships
of intimacy need be relationships of affection, love and candour. Rather
physical proximity is only the helpful condition to a deep affection and
growth; the partners in the relationships must themselves take advantage
of the first type of intimacy and (continuously) create the second kind of
intimacy—and thereby reach a perfection held out to each one as the
reward of a relationship of affection, candour and love. This essay intends
to extract from the New Testament what can help create, develop and
sustain this second sense of intimacy; the New Testament has much to
offer on two levels—that of reflective insight and that of personal relationships. Let us first consider the reflective insights of the New
Testament relative to intimacy.

Most people accept an interpersonal relationship of intimacy as normal
and desirable; its absence is judged as a loss, as a failure, and as an
abnormality. The New Testament, together with the Old, has intimacy as
its foundational notion. Its thrust, beyond all images, laws, ideals, is
towards unity of each person with God. In this sense, the struggle of each
person for fulfilment through intimacy—and the absolute conviction that
his is a just and necessary struggle—is affirmed in the Bible. And this
affirmation is, in a loose sense, revelatory about a human being's inner-
most longings—it affirms that God is constantly and historically ever
trying to create and maintain intimacy with each creature, and such an
intimacy that the images used in the Bible serve only to excite a person's
imagination to dream the seemingly impossible.

A second and fundamental contribution of the New Testament has to
do with value. Many people understand that the New Testament reveals
God but they do not fully realise that the revelation about God is also a

revelation about themselves. Specifically, when Jesus dies on the cross as expressive of God's love for us, this reveals the worth or value, in God's eyes, of those for whom Jesus dies. Paul's famous insight applies here— that among humans, who would die for a friend? who for an enemy? and yet God does what human beings are not inclined to do 'for their own kind'. And so, one begins to reflect. How much worth do I put on any, every human being? What does God reveal to me through His sacrifice—and not only sacrifice; He created, persists in offering Himself always, and prepares an eternity of joy through intimate union with each and every creature? In the struggle to develop union, love, affection— 'intimacy'—it is fundamental to stabilise in one's mind the deserved esteem and true value of one's partner. Few systems of thought (if any) present such a noble and consoling assessment of a human being and the reason for this uniqueness lies in the fact that for once human value is defined, not by other humans, but by God.

Moreover, there is a breadth and grandness to this revelation which puts things into a better perspective. Intimacy often flounders in indi- viduality and considers it an enemy. Yet individuality, in New Testament terms, is of the essence of human existence. Each of us is a story before and beyond relationships: each has a pre-history in the mind of God, is the object of untold graces, and intimate, 'divine union', is called to decisions in a privacy of fear and uncertainty and has an eternal future to hope for, to secure. The divine right, the radical divine appeal to each person indicates a sovereignty which perplexes the drive towards union, assimilation, identification. Though the New Testament does not solve the multiple instances of tension between the desire for intimacy and the search for self into eternity, it lays bare the reality which is the make-up of each of us and this provides a basic definition of any human being sought out as a partner.

The revelation of the New Testament about human nature suggests two further thoughts. First, the New Testament presents a framework about reality. It defines the goals, origins, and characteristics of human beings; it gives orientation to the puzzling presence of evil, to the danger of eternal suffering; most significantly in the context of this essay, it defines a human being as sinner and saint, totally dependent on God for the ultimate victory over evil. Such a comprehensive statement, if the New Testament is right, reveals the reality in which life can and will function; to accept it is to accept reality, but to reject it is to doom in advance relationships built on false 'reality'.

Secondly, and briefly, one's partner in intimacy, if he or she be a New Testament adherent, is intelligible, explicable through knowledge of the New Testament. A believer is committed to a way of life and a self—and world—view consonant with the New Testament. If knowledge is a means to greater intimacy, the New Testament, in its revelation, is a strong help to understanding any partner who is a believer (however lukewarm) in the New Testament.

A final paragraph in this first, or theoretical section should emphasise the New Testament's insistence as to the essence of human life: to love God and to love one's neighbour. Whatever may be the dangers and successes of intimate union, the New Testament is convinced that love is the ultimate driving power to successful intimacy. The 'Golden Rule' or 'turning the other cheek' or the law 'against divorce' or the command to 'obey those who have authority over you'—whatever particular segment of the New Testament one chooses—this is an attempt to specify what love involves, and to indicate what is the way, in God's mind, to one's greatest fulfilment.

The New Testament, then, offers foundational insights about union and intimacy. It also offers examples of such intimacy which are provocative and instructive; of special interest for this essay are the lives of Jesus and Paul.

The Gospels, it is generally agreed today, do not offer primarily a biography of Jesus; the evangelists had specific problems, often generated by their audiences, to deal with, and the many stories of Jesus' life were selected, edited and organised with a view to solving these problems. Yet, secondarily, and not unexpectedly, there are glimpses of Jesus' relationships with others, and it is worth considering these if for no other reason than to be convinced that even in 'the best of worlds', intimacy as a desirable and productive state can be difficult, can be inexplicably limited and must always be worked at.

One of the most striking relationships in the Gospels is that of Jesus with His Father. We have come to accept them, each as God, as equals. But it is clear from His language and His experiences that Jesus consistently had to sacrifice (there is no other word for it) to maintain His relationship. Underneath the sovereignty of the Gospel Jesus is an awareness that every time He spoke candidly, to explain Himself and His opinions, He was asking for more trouble. At one time He thought it would be good if 'trouble' were to be removed from Him, that His Father be less demanding. As one report has it, he cried for being forsaken. But this tension in the relationship did not kill it. Hand in hand with this tension went nights of prayer, of intimacy—and Jesus' relationship grew productive until it resulted in resurrection. This relationship is not typical of us in many ways; yet, it is remarkable in that its consistency and growth went through difficult and threatening times. The relationship was strained and yet the maintenance of the relationship created a bond ever the stronger and ever a motive for not letting anything dissolve it.

A second difficult relationship for Jesus was His relationship with His disciples. Once again the data we possess has been altered, adjusted, moulded; yet some aspects are surely decipherable. Jesus may have known His disciples for two years and some months (as the Johannine material would have it) or only about sixteen months (as the Markan material, the basis of the Matthean and Lucan stories, indicates). At the end of that period of time, marked by ignorance, bickering, fascination, frustration, loyalty and disloyalty, Jesus could feel comfort at having lost no one but the Son of Perdition. There is no way of assessing these relationships and their motivations properly. Surely miracles helped, as did more so wise words; but weariness, rancour, travel, futilities certainly took their toll. What kept the relationship together for so long and, finally, forever? It is difficult and even rash for the exegete to move in this area, but the candour, sharing, honesty and affection, begun in selection and continued in physical nearness, together with the truth—all this seems to have entered into it.

A final reference, in regard to Jesus' life, is more general: it embraces relationships for which we have little data. Imagination (not unreasonable) has done much to develop the relationship of Jesus and Mary. Little data though there be, the intimacy between them seems to have grown uninterrupted and filled with trust. Similarly the constant friendship of Jesus with Martha, Mary, Lazarus asks explanation; there really is none given, yet the tears of Jesus and the friendship and hospitality of the Lazarus household show the perdurance of a friendship even when friendship with Jesus perils one's life.

The glimpses of how Jesus and his friends loved one another show that the command to love one's neighbour dictates a love which is human, affective, emotional as well as eager for the good of the other. These relationships witness the New Testament truth: love is what a human being should do—and, conversely, love is what a human being should look for.

The Gospels, then, present images of intimate relationships, a variety of relationships indeed, but related in their diversity through the one principle of love. St Paul, however, presents more than a glimpse and offers more than a principle of relationship. His letters in many parts are part of an actual creative effort at maintaining union. They represent situations based on past intimacy but in danger of disruption and failure. If anywhere Christianity is human, i.e., if anywhere there is an interweaving of doctrine and personal love in such wise that maintenance of love, respect, unselfishness, understanding is integral to the preservation of the correct understanding of God's action in Christ, it is in the Pauline letters. No one struggles for love like Paul, no one is so desperate in his plea for trust, understanding and fidelity than is Paul; his letters reflect this precisely because they are instruments in his effort to keep intimate union alive. His motivation is, it is true, not just the desire to be loved—Paul is convinced that a closing of one's heart to him is the sure way to abandonment of Christ in his deepest significance. But there are texts which step outside of this motivation, texts which attest to Paul's own affection for his readers, his personal need for their inspiration and consolation as well as his conviction that he has much to contribute to the happiness of others.

One can cite individual tests for quite some time to elucidate Paul's often serpentine thought patterns responding to the psychological needs, fears, demand of his audience. But a general and rousing encouragement is more in order, an encouragement to look through the Pauline letters not as doctrinal documents or as religious literature 'speaking to me', but as correspondence revealing some two-thousand year-old moments in a relationship between a brilliant, poetic, not very attractive, fanatical genius and a community of some poor, some rich, some ignorant, some intelligent, all unsure and in need of guidance in their new commitment. These letters show the value of candour and assurances of love by interpreting past deeds, of sincerity in promises; they also reveal failings, some moral, some psychological, some remediable, some unhappily not. But more than any other literature there is visible in the Pauline letters a mirror of human relationships trying to establish themselves as founded upon and inspired by God in Christ; this literature reflects not merely principles for intimate living but the actual effort to live an intimate relationship in some kind of marriage between Christian ideals and human weakness.

A pause is in order, a pause to recommend specially a reading of Paul's second letter to the Corinthians. Careful analysis shows that Paul tried very hard to maintain a relation of more than ordinary friendliness with the Corinthians; *Second Corinthians* is for the greater part an excellent window for the reader to watch a poignant and delicate drama unfold. Consider carefully the sum effect of 2:17; 10:1,7,10,12,18; 12:11; 13:3; each test is actually a type of accusation or criticism of Paul who is distant (in Ephesus) and unable to defend himself except by this tardy letter. Consider how any couple or group would reel under the kinds of accusations to which Paul has been subjected in Corinth. Paul's partners in intimacy have forgotten the claims Paul made in the ninth chapter of *First Corinthians*: he had a right to be loved in the way he loved others, but he gave up all his rights to help them find and hold onto the greatest happiness. It is true that Paul is not, for many, an engaging character who elicits sympathy easily, and it is also true that the parameters of his relationship are not the same as those of married people or of other types of intimate relationships; but it is hard to find a mirror to reflect better the enduring threats to friendship and affection which many people suffer than the experience of Paul, and it is equally difficult to find a nobler, more generous solution to this struggle than the principles and ideals of Paul.

And what is said in regard to the Corinthian relationship can be said also about Paul's relationship with the Philippians and Galatians. Paul exhibits patience, shows anger, consoles, incites, praises, rebukes. One of the great lessons that can be drawn from the reading of the New Testament, particularly of the Pauline literature, is the constant real-isation of the New Testament's actual practice of love. Inevitably, people will define love or intimate living in terms which are presumably from the New Testament but which actually are culturally developed preferences. In this scheme rebuke, anger, silence are considered as acts of non-love. Yet, when one turns to the New Testament (and to the Old, too) one sees how the many emotions and responses involved in intimacy issue as part of love. In this regard the New Testament is well worth reading, for it integrates love and human interaction in a way few theories have ever done.

Before leaving the Pauline literature, a word is in order regarding what is perhaps the most intimate of human relationships, marriage. Little is said about marriage throughout the New Testament; Paul says the most on the subject. Brief though his treatment is, one cannot but be impressed by his offering to a married couple as a model the relationship of the Church and Christ. One must transcend the culturally determined roles of man and wife, but, that done, the depth of commitment, sacrifice, unity suggested in Ephesians 5:22-23 is unparalleled.

The ending of this essay signals a need for distinction. It is clear from Scripture analyses over the past centuries that the New Testament is not a book on psychology. It does deal with love, even containing one of the most memorable descriptions of love (I Cor. 13) ever written; it also deals with anger, hatred, murder, lust, selfishness—and it treats of obedience, fidelity, despair and reality. But the New Testament cannot substitute for psychiatry or psychology on the level of techniques for self-knowledge, for better communication, for understanding the psyche, especially in terms of myriad influences and the limits of healing.

But just as there is no way in which the New Testament can substitute for psychiatry in its techniques and scientific contributions, there is no way in which any of the social or personal sciences can replace the vision and insight of the New Testament. True, the New Testament is a book the power of which depends on faith, but no science would ever make claims which could supplant those of the New Testament and not equally depend on faith. The New Testament, in the question of intimacy, confirms the need for affection, candour, love; indeed, it insists, through the use of its most profound image, that union is the sole way to happiness, fulfilment and peace. It offers the principle of selflessness which, contradictorily, saves one's life. It insists, at first glance foolishly perhaps, that life is not fulfilled by loving God alone; happiness includes love of one's neighbour. Many of the relationships of the New Testament express the ways people have nobly tried to establish and maintain intimate relationships. The parameters of the relationships (Lord to disciple, teacher to convert) often do not coincide with our own personal relationships. But our viewing of these relationships and the realisation of the struggles and techniques used to keep these relationships alive and always under the noblest of motives and sentiments—this is most consoling and instructive.

Mary Durkin

Intimacy and Marriage: Continuing the Mystery of Christ and the Church

A FEW years ago our eighteen-year-old daughter proposed her solution to the problems of broken homes. Married couples should, in her opinion, wait until they have been married at least two years before they begin to plan for a child. By this time they would know whether or not the marriage was going to work; and they would thus avoid subjecting children to the traumas of divorce if they discovered they could not live together. With the experience of twenty years of marriage we were quick to point out to her that even after two years a couple are not able to predict accurately the future of their relationship. Unfortunately, within a year we were able to prove our point. The marriages of three close friends, all of whom had been married over fifteen years, ended. In each instance there were children born at a time when the partners imagined they would remain married 'until death do us part'.

But there is a grain of truth to the idea that the agreement entered into on the wedding day is not, for many couples, of sufficient depth to constitute a sacramental marriage, that is a union which will, over the possible fifty years that the couple could be married, somehow reflect the mystery of Christ and the Church. The questions which confront us, if we acknowledge this, are: how do we determine what kind of a commitment must be made to have a sacramental marriage, and how can we determine when such a commitment is finally achieved?

In order to examine the issues posed by these questions theological discussion of the sacrament of marriage must move from the heavy emphasis on law found in canon law discussions of marriage to an investigation of the phenomenon of marriage as an event (not just the initial contract) which spans a long period of time. In the more advanced

74

cultures of the 1970s this period of time is of sufficient length to ensure that the personalities of the individuals will undergo many changes which will have a profound effect on the life of the union. We need to examine marriage as a concrete reality lived out by real human beings, undergoing the complexities of human existence. We need to analyse these unions and determine how it is possible for them to participate in the mystery of Christ and the Church.

To begin this discussion here we will first examine marriage as a social and religious institution both in the past and in the present. We will explore how a commitment to develop the potential for intimacy might be the dimension of the manifold symbol of marriage which allows it to continue to be a sacrament in a world that no longer needs monogamous marriage for economic survival; and we will suggest some pastoral implications of our claim that the potential for intimacy and the actual achievement of intimacy give marriage in advanced technological societies its sacramental possibility—its ability to stand for the relationship of Christ and the Church while at the same time participating in that union and creatively continuing the union. We will limit our discussion to marriage in advanced technological societies, fully aware that there are other concrete experiences of marriage, but finding the situation in advanced societies to be such that the intimacy question is most apparent there.

SACRAMENTS AS CREATIVE SYMBOLS

Before analysing the sacramental dimension of marriage we need to set forth a brief explanation of how certain events in the life of humankind can be said to symbolise the mystery of God and His relationship to His people. The efficacy of a sacrament, from a process point of view, depends upon a correct intuition at work in interpretation of the basic symbols of the sacrament.[1] For a symbol, which is manifold, to become a sacrament, the Spirit of Jesus must be authentically at work and the symbol must function with a society (the Church) as its interpreter. In addition, the symbol of a sacrament must really participate in the Jesus-event as it actually occurred, and it must also participate in the contemporary event which it is said to embody. In other words, 'A Sacrament will not make the Jesus-event present if the symbol's form of definiteness is not truly *there* in the Jesus-event as well as *here* in the contemporary situation'.[2]

Whitehead maintains that the expressive sign is also creative when it elicits the intuition which interprets it as long as there is something there to be elicited.[3] In other words, for a sacrament to work *ex opere operato* it is necessary for a Christian subjectivity to exist so that a manifold symbol may become an event which allows the Jesus-event creatively to invade the contemporary scene. Marriage 'stands for' many things. Only when a Christian community is able to uncover or 'intuit' a certain connectedness between the real lived experience of marriage and the mystery of the union of Christ and the Church are Christians able to experience marriage as a creative sign. If there were no possibility of uncovering this connectedness, the Christian community would have difficulty maintaining its claim that marriage is a sacrament.

But we must avoid the view that marriage is a static institution which has not undergone changes throughout human history. For then we would see connectedness only in marital unions which are identical with those of the time of the early Church and would miss the opportunity to explore the richness of marriages contracted at other times in history.

MARRIAGE AS A SOCIAL AND RELIGIOUS INSTITUTION

Monogamous marriage is a relative newcomer to the scene of male-female relations for *Homo sapiens*. Although there are indications that every human society has acknowledged sexual differentiation and controlled sexual behaviour through role assignments and taboos, the idea of one man and one woman forming an exclusive union until the death of one partner has not been the natural pattern throughout human history. And the idea of monogamous marriage founded on love and the desire for intimacy is very recent in the 40,000-year history of *Homo sapiens*. Indeed, it is only in the 200 years since the industrial revolution that a need for economic survival of the individual, the family and the society at large has not had to be the primary motive for marriage. And it has only been in the last twenty years that conditions in a few of the advanced technological societies have freed women from concern for survival and allowed them to consider marriage an experience which allows for personal growth and development as well as the opportunity for motherhood.

Yet the event of monogamous marriage (not just the ceremony, but the continuous living out of the union) has held an attraction for religious leaders in the Judeo-Christian culture since at least the time of the earliest tales of creation recorded in Genesis. Hosea's faithfulness to Gomer is a symbol of Yahweh's love for Israel. The joys of intimacy described in Song of Songs, if not originally meant to signify the joy of the covenant between Yahweh and Israel, came to symbolise this by the time of its inclusion in the Old Testament canon. Paul tells the Ephesians that the union of a husband and wife is a mystery that has many implications, but which he says 'applies to Christ and the Church' (Eph. 5:32). Since an event can only symbolise that to which it has a certain connectedness, it is obvious that both the Old Testament community and the young Church saw the union of two in one flesh demanding faithfulness and love and as a source of joy for those who were committed to the union.

Prior to the religious interpretation, however, society needed tó regulate male and female relations, not merely to limit the sexual activities of its members, but more importantly to establish protection for the mother-child bond during the years of infancy. Once a male was acknowledged as the father of the infant, he would have the responsibility of assuming the well-being of both mother and child. In return he would be assured of offspring to help care for his property and to carry on after his death. In short, marriage began in response to the need for economic survival, and it offered both the male and the female certain rewards in return for their co-operation in the bearing and rearing of children. Within these types of unions many people, undoubtedly, found love and intimacy as is indicated by the religious writers' use of marriage as a symbol of God's love. But the goal of love and intimacy was not the primary reason for marriage, as is evidenced by the customs of arranged marriages and dowries.

Still, when the ancient Israelite writers, Jesus, and Paul looked at marriage in their day they saw these unions calling forth fidelity and love which hint at the fidelity and love of God. When the Catholic Church pronounced marriage to be one of the seven sacraments it officially interpreted the manifold symbol of marriage as a creative sign of the faithfulness of God and the mystery of Christ and the Church. Marriage 'until death do us part' is seen as a sign of hope that love never dies even when it appears to have faded away. When the Church intuits this meaning in marriage it is also encouraging those who marry to participate in the symbol and partake of the grace which is promised.

But the reasons for marrying have changed greatly over the last 200 years, and in present-day, post-industrial societies we no longer find the society needing monogamous marriage to assure the continuation of the society, the economic survival of the mother and child, or the continuation of family property. So the sacramental theologian must examine why people marry to determine if marriage continues to be a symbol which the Church can intuit to have a certain connectedness to the mystery of Christ and the Church.

POTENTIAL FOR INTIMACY

Most people, including Christians, in advanced technological societies would maintain that they marry because they are in love. Few people marry anymore simply to have children or to increase or protect their economic status. Yet it is very difficult for most people to articulate what love means and specifically what they hope to gain from their particular marriage relationship. In the type of society created by advanced cultures, people are free to arrange their own marriages and often free to terminate those marriages which do not keep alive the 'in love' feeling. Civil society has become increasingly more tolerant of divorce since it no longer views marriage as necessary for economic survival. When people are free to marry at will, the question arises as to whether they should bother to stay married when they are no longer in love. While the Church continues to see marriage as a sign of the faithfulness of Yahweh and Jesus, many other segments of society view the life-long commitment of two people to each other as too demanding. Some maintain that this kind of commitment is impossible.

As the literature on human growth and development explores the various stages of growth and development which people who are living longer and having smaller families undergo in the course of their lives, arguments, both pro and con, have developed concerning life-long commitment. Those who are against monogamous marriage argue that we must be open to possibilities of change in our lives. A relationship entered into in our early twenties may be an obstacle to the potential we discover when we reach our late thirties or forties or fifties. If we are to be true to the development of our human potential we must reject such obstacles and move ahead, finding new love relationships that meet our needs at a particular time. Generally this view favours serial monogamy.

On the pro-commitment side an argument is made for the need for continuity in a rapidly changing society. It is only when one is able to make the commitment 'to concrete affiliations and partnerships and to develop the ethical strength to abide by such commitments, even though they may call for significant sacrifice and compromise'[4] that one demonstrates a capacity for intimacy. It is this capacity for intimacy which, in the fidelities and commitments it evokes, reinforces our identity and assures a continuity between the bride and groom at age twenty-three and the senior citizen grandparents at age seventy. In a relationship of intimacy, love is a decision that in some aspects of our personalities we will not change, that we will stick by certain commitments.

A further argument can be made that the psycho-social survival of a society depends on marriage and a family life which will encourage its members to take the risk involved in forming intimate relationships. According to Erik Erikson it is only when people are able to develop their capacity for intimacy that true genitality can fully develop. In turn it is true genitality which encourages the sort of satisfactory sex relations that 'makes sex less obsessive, overcompensation less necessary, sadistic controls superfluous'.[5]

Leisure class societies, which have given their young the opportunity of a moratorium which allows them to determine their own identities, create some problems for their young adults when they begin to consider marriage. If a marriage choice is made before an identity is developed, it is often a choice which will not allow an intimate relationship to develop. Since, for many young adults the moratorium is extending into the early twenties, marriage choices are being made before the individuals have achieved a balance between a sense of coherence and a sense of identity confusion with the balance favouring coherence; in short, before an identity has been formed. Without this sense of coherence it is difficult for a person to promise the fidelity necessary to achieve intimacy.

In addition to fidelity, intimacy requires a love that is more than a feeling love. It must be a mature love in which will is joined to feeling, in which partners give up the tentativeness of former relationships and vow themselves to a constancy which, in effect, acknowledges that some doors to other opportunities will remain forever closed. The choice for intimacy is a choice which will determine the future possible identities of the partners. As Erikson points out, it is not good for an individual to make an important commitment while his/her identity is still in an immature stage.

This does not necessarily means that all marriage choices made before a certain age are going to lead to failures in the relationship. Some people are able to adjust to a marriage and continue to grow in their own sense of self, but this will be extremely difficult for those who do not have a firm grasp of their own identity.

Canon lawyers involved in marriage tribunals are seeing the psychological inability to commit oneself to a particular other person as an impediment to a *legally* valid sacramental marriage. While allowing that a couple might have entered a union in good faith, the tribunals are annulling marriages for psychological impediments. They are not claiming to identify the sacramental basis of marriage, but they are claiming that one or both parties was legally unable to make the commitment called for in a valid sacramental marriage.

From the perspective of marriage as a sign or symbol, it is also true that at the time a couple agrees to a marriage contract they are often not ready to make a commitment to develop their capacity for intimacy. Even when both partners are able to make this commitment, it is necessary that they renew their promise continuously during their marriage, especially during the critical stages of personality development. When marriage is seen as a participation in the continuation of the Jesus-event in contemporary society, a couple finds encouragement to exercise continually the creative aspects of their relationship in both physical and psychological generativity, which in turn can lessen the burdens that might occur at certain critical moments in a marriage. Many couples who marry prior to developing their capacity for intimacy can be encouraged to develop this capacity so that their marriage will also participate in the Jesus-event.

SOME PASTORAL IMPLICATIONS

The pastoral implications of the position that contemporary marriages, which are a place for developing one's capacity for intimacy, are symbolic of the mystery of Christ and the Church and are, therefore, valid sacraments, are many. In concluding we will consider three:

1. Preparation for a sacramental marriage begins in infancy as the child begins to confront and master the critical stages of life. Adolescence, when the teenager gets a second opportunity to work at identity formation and begins to create his/her own identity, is another critical period of marriage preparation. Pastoral efforts should concentrate on helping people create family environments which contribute to the formation of positive identities. Young adults should be encouraged to evaluate their identity development before planning marriage.

2. Life cycle theories emphasise that commitment to intimacy demands constant renewal. Pastoral programmes are needed which encourage couples to deal constructively with the problems they encounter through continual reference to the sacramental nature of their commitment. For those who are not familiar with life cycle theories, a good starting point would be a programme which addresses the critical stages of adult life. Commitment to another entails the risk of involvement in the life of another, and this requires an understanding of how the other's growth and development affects one's own development.

3. Commitment to another involves, along with the risk of involvement, the risk of rejection. Pastoral programmes are needed to meet the needs of those who take the risk and experience failure. Marriage, more than any other sacrament, can fail to be connected to the Jesus-event through the rejection of one person. The Church community must help those who have been rejected in their attempt at intimacy, as well as those who have not been able to take the risk of intimacy.

In conclusion we acknowledge that the Christian community (the Church) can intuit a connectedness between the fidelity and love needed to achieve intimacy in contemporary marriage and the mystery of Christ and the Church; and, therefore, can legitimately continue to consider marriage a sacrament. It must also recognise that many particular marital unions, even between baptised Christians, do not and cannot achieve a capacity for intimacy.

Notes

1. For more on a process understanding of sacrament, see B. Lee *The Becoming of the Church* (New York 1974).
2. *Ibid*. p. 213.
3. A. Whitehead *Religion in the Making* (Cleveland 1960) p. 128.
4. E. Erikson *Childhood and Society* (New York 1963) p. 263.
5. *Ibid*. p. 265.

Walter Heim

Religious Practice within the Family: A Contribution to the Theology of Intimate Belonging in the Light of Popular Beliefs and Customs in the Past

I COME from a lower middle-class family which, although not wealthy, could not be counted among the really poor. Despite the economic crisis of the 1930s, I was happy, and basic to my happiness was the sense of belonging within my family. My clearest memories are of family celebrations (of Christmas, of first communions and birthdays) and of going to church and singing together. Later, we would listen to the radio and gramophone and discuss what we had heard. Although we weren't rich, we gave a relatively large amount to charity—it wasn't infrequent that people in need would be invited to eat with us—as well as to the missions. The gifts we sent to the 'pagan children' and the cards of thanks and acknowledgement which followed, made a deep impression on me. Emboldened by this and by missionary magazines and calendars, at the age of twelve I was ready to exchange the security of my family circle for a mission school. There too I found a sense of belonging, a feeling of familiarity, engendered chiefly by the school celebrations of Christmas and St Nicholas and the torch-lit processions on the feast of Christ the King.

I have mentioned all this because an individual's experience is often the best way of illustrating the factors that can be significant in creating an atmosphere of belonging within the family unit. Shared values and assumptions, verbal and trans-verbal communication are essential if a social group is to remain cohesive. Symbols and custom can be decisive in promoting a sense of belonging. An example of this is the practice of saying grace before and after meals—a custom upheld by far more families than one might expect and something which astonished a group of school children from Geneva when visiting families in Lucerne.

Religious practice and belief—an essential constituent of popular culture[1]—is one of the most important factors in engendering an atmosphere of belonging which has a religious feel about it. Sociological studies of the role of popular religious beliefs and observances show, among other things, the way in which the Church's festivals punctuate the seasons of the year and the lives of the people, providing focal points of celebration. And in this way they make use of and so conserve vestiges of an older culture. For reasons of space I am obliged to confine my discussion to an examination of those celebrations and festivals which are of particular significance to the family.

1. POPULAR RELIGIOUS PRACTICE IN THE PREINDUSTRIAL FAMILY

The peasant and artisan families of preindustrial Europe were profoundly affected by prevailing religious and moral norms, common methods of production and the discipline and culture of the village community. Socio-economic factors and strict moral sanctions defined family relationships and determined the quality of life. Love and intimacy played a much smaller role. Nevertheless, there was often deep feeling. The vehicles for this were such religious celebrations as the attendance by the whole family at *Rorate* Masses [a *Rorate* Mass is a white votive Mass of Our Lady celebrated during the season of Advent in certain parts of Germany *(translator's note)*] or their full participation in the Midnight Mass at Christmas. This latter was always a red-letter day for families and could bring balm to the most conflict-ridden.

Christmas cribs were first introduced into the home in the eighteenth century. These were built in the peasant's or craftsman's home and they often involved the whole family in weeks of co-operative labour to ensure they were ready for the Christmas-eve devotions. In Oberpfalz [a part of Bavaria to the north-west of Regensburg *(translator's note)*] the family would crouch in the straw around the crib until it was time for the Midnight Mass.[2] In Montlingen (St Gallen) on Christmas night the striking of the great clock would mark the time for the family to say a 'psalter' (the joyful, sorrowful and glorious mysteries of the Rosary).

In Lenggries and Kachel (southern Bavaria) embers from the Easter fire are still taken to the people's houses and used to light the family hearth.[3] But it is only in parts of Austria that the old custom of the family

Easter fires (which had once been observed throughout Middle-Europe) has been preserved: each year they are lit to the singing of Easter hymns by embers taken from the church fire.[4]

In many areas special baskets of Easter lamb and eggs to be eaten at the mid-day meal would first be taken to the church to be blessed. It was at this time too that the highly prized 'Maundy Thursday eggs' were eaten by the father and children. This was a ritual that expressed and strengthened the patriarchal father's authority over his household and extended family, for the eating of the 'Maundy Thursday eggs' ensured that during the year to come no one would stray from the family fold.[5]

2. CUSTOM AND RELIGIOUS PRACTICE IN THE BOURGEOIS FAMILY

The emergence of the bourgeois family in the eighteenth and nineteenth centuries coincided with an increasingly romanticised conception of family life. The growing prosperity of some sections of the population meant that more money was available for the celebration of wedding anniversaries and birthdays.[6] This new romantic attitude is particularly apparent in the feasts and celebrations that centred on children.

At Christmas, trees decorated with tinsel, lights and presents for the children, assumed a central place in the celebrations. At first, Christmas trees were confined to the houses of the aristocracy but by the beginning of the twentieth century, their use was widespread and they began to appear for the first time in churches. On Christmas eve the presents would be put beside the tree and covered with a cloth, while the family gathered round to recite poems, sing carols and listen to the father read aloud from the Christmas gospel. Only when this was over were the children given their presents.[7]

Christmas was very much a family festival and it served—consciously or unconsciously—to reinforce the father's authority and to maintain discipline within the family. Christmas, celebrated in the best room or parlour around the candle-lit tree, was a patriarchal occasion on which the presence of all family members was compulsory. They gathered together, temporarily shut off from the world outside, acknowledging the authority of the father and the strength of the ties that bound them together. 'When the first candles begin to burn, the family assemble, conscious of their intimacy, their exclusivity and their common sense of belonging. They were jealously insistent too that sons and daughters normally living away from home should return to the family circle for the occasion.'[8]

With the emergence of the bourgeois family, Easter too developed into a festival particularly associated with children. Easter-egg hunts became an established tradition and the Easter hare [The Easter hare, like the English Easter rabbit, hides the eggs which the children hunt for on Easter morning. In the same way as angels or figures of the Christ child are hung from the branches of Christmas trees, in south Germany tiny painted wooden hares are hung from the blossom and spring flowers which decorate the houses at Easter *(translator's note)*.] acquired a romanticised symbolic significance as the bringer of gifts (the Easter equivalent of the Christ child at Christmas).

3. CUSTOM AND OBSERVANCE WITHIN THE NUCLEAR FAMILY

Social isolation and high geographical mobility have transformed the family. The large extended family unit of preindustrial Europe has been succeeded by the nuclear family, and in the process the nuclear family has become an 'intimate group' where deep feelings become concentrated and intensified. The history of 'White Sunday' is a typical example of the way in which the family has appropriated and transformed traditional customs.

'White Sunday', a collective celebration for first communicants, is first documented in Munich in 1661 where the festivities were conducted with characteristic Baroque pomp and ceremony. By the nineteenth century these children's processions were being organised on a parochial basis throughout most of German-speaking Europe. At the turn of the century the family began to interest itself in White Sunday, although in rural areas it was not until the early 1930s that White-Sunday celebrations became a family-based occasion.[9] During my youth in the diocese of St Gallen, it was customary for each child to choose a 'communion partner' with whom to process into the church. Poor children usually chose richer ones as partners for they would then spend their first-communion day in the home of a family wealthier than their own. First-communion days have become more egalitarian in recent years and the church ceremony is followed immediately by a family celebration at home. 'From the point of view of internal religious profit, it is a positive advantage that collective first-communion celebrations have been abandoned in favour of an individual first communion, received within the family circle, quite apart from the fact that an early communion is now considered appropriate.'[10]

As well as Christmas, the modern nuclear family has created a 'second family feast'. It has long been the custom for whole families to take part in the church visit to the cemetery on the afternoon of All Saints' Day; but now, in an age when children are leaving home earlier than before, it has become traditional for sons and daughters to return home on All Saints' Day (or on the following Sunday) to remember the dead and thereby incidentally to acknowledge ties of both family and village community. At Christmas too, it is customary to decorate the family graves with tiny

Christmas trees, evergreen and candles.[11] These are all typical examples of customs developed by the nuclear family.

4. COMPULSION AND FREEDOM

In the bourgeois family, Christmas was very much a children's festival. In the modern nuclear family (irrespective of social class), it has been turned into a feast for the entire family. Where there had once been only a festive meal on Christmas Day itself, there was now a family meal on Christmas Eve too, to which were added other similar family festivities around the candle-lit tree on St Stephen's Day and at New Year. 'The way Christmas is celebrated in the twentieth century, shows that the family is regarded as a natural and harmonious association. It is a place of retreat from the harshness of day-to-day life, a place without conflicts, because one feels safe there.'[12]

From this it is clear why all family members are obliged to spend Christmas at home and why it is forbidden (at least on Christmas Day) to leave the family circle to visit friends or to go to a pub or restaurant.

The smaller the family, the greater is the pressure on its individual members. Children around puberty experience this most directly, for it conflicts with their struggle to emancipate themselves from the religious and social values of their elders and their desire to create a 'sub-culture' of their own.[13] The obligation to take part in the family Christmas celebration represents for many an unwarranted compulsion: they are obliged to express gratitude and to be in harmony with their surroundings. They may register their protest by deliberately staying away—a course of action that can lead to bitter family tragedies.

This kind of pressure seems hardly an appropriate means of engendering an atmosphere of family trust and closeness today! Certainly the spiritual emptiness and the sort of neurosis that comes from a sense of futility, experienced by many young people, are caused by the lack of strong and effective family bonds. Family customs and traditions charged with genuine feeling can help to counteract this, but they too, can be counter-productive, particularly when too much emotion is invested in specific feast-days and occasions such as Christmas.

'A rejection of the old and traditional ways of celebrating Christmas, itself implies that new forms of celebration are needed. But to accept these, "to say yes to celebration", requires a faith and a confidence that is no longer self-evident. It is not surprising that Christians (both young and old) who experience their faith as uncertain and developing (as opposed to achieved and unquestioned), will feel battered and over-taxed by even the new forms of celebration, which they perceive as a deep-seated and terror-laden emotional threat.'[14]

To stay away from home altogether or simply to watch television, is no solution to these problems. Young people often experience far greater pressure and far worse terrors in their 'own milieu' outside the family circle.

The psychologist B. Grom suggests that the meaning of religious celebrations, and the observances and prohibitions that these imply, should be discussed openly within the family. 'The new "yes to celebration" can contribute to a real Christmas culture, only if celebration is combined with a readiness to discuss the implications of belief. It is only when we seek to be open, that Christmas can assume genuine meaning. A free and tolerant discussion of beliefs is needed to ease the painful emotional pressure that can be experienced when family festivities simply follow on from a meditation in church or on the radio. Personal, individually formulated prayers of thanks or petition, music or carol singing, can develop out of the discussion, and the family celebrations should follow automatically, without a break or a sense that the "spiritual" and the "festive" parts of the evening are separate and unconnected.'[15]

I have discussed the celebration of Christmas at some length. It is, however, no more than one example among many of the importance of religion in accentuating celebration within the family. The practice of saying grace before and after meals is an example of how the process can work within daily family life.

On no account should the family fail to seize every opportunity of using traditional celebrations, symbol and play so as to create high points in family life, to provide an atmosphere of intimacy, belonging and trust and to bring order and meaning (*kosmos*) to an otherwise threatening chaos. To vary the title-phrase of an essay by M. Goepfert entitled 'Der Glaube lebt von vertrauten Worten' (Faith lives through Familiar Words),[16] one can say, on the basis of research into popular religious beliefs and customs, that the family lives through rituals of belonging, and particularly through traditional family celebrations which improve the quality of family life.

Our attitudes have changed in recent years. We used to speak of a theology of crisis which perceived belief as uncertainty, as risk, as paradox, as decision and as a break with theological tradition. But we are progressing towards a theology of intimate belonging which will emphasise again the importance of the individual's integration into his own life history, into the collective life history of the community and, above all, into the life history of the family group. 'Belief is made real when it is historically mediated; it only survives and grows as an integral part of the language, games and traditions, acquired (above all in the family) in the process of education and self-realisation.'[17]

Translated by Miranda Chaytor

Notes

1. Cf. D. Yoder 'Toward a definition of folk religion' *Western Folklore* 33 (1974) pp. 2-15 (symposium on Folks Religion which includes a discussion of 'Folk religion: the folk-cultural dimension of religion' and 'the religious dimension on folk-culture').

2. On *Rorate* Masses see J. Schlicht 'Das Engelamt' *Bayerisch Land und Bayerisch Volk* (Staubing 1875); on cribs see W. A. Widmann and W. Sitta *Die Wahrhaft göttliche Komedi: Hauskrippen im Stiftland* (Regensburg 1976).

3. G. Kapfhammer *Brauchtum in den Alpenländern* (Munich 1977) p. 206.

4. M. Zender 'Glaube und Brauch, Fest und Spiel' in G. Wiegelmann, M. Zender, G. Heilfurth *Volkskunde* (Berlin 1977) p. 143.

5. F. Hager and H. Heyn *Drudenhax und Allelujawasser: Volksbrauch im Jahreslauf* (Rosenheim 1975) p. 167.

6. M. Zender *op. cit.* p. 192.

7. *Op. cit.* p. 146 f.

8. I. Weber-Kellermann 'Weihnachtsbräuche als Akte innenfamiliärer Kommunikation' in H. Hausinger and E. Moser Rath (ed.) *Direkte Kommunikation und Massenkommunikation* (Tübingen 1976) p. 175.

9. Cf. N. Henrichs *Kult und Brauchtum im Kirchenjahr* (Düsseldorf 1967) p. 49.

10. *Op. cit.* p. 50.

11. H. Trümpy 'Entstehung und Ausbreitung eines neuen Brauches', 1977 Annual Report of the Schweizerische Geisteswissenschaftliche Gesellschaft (Bern 1978) pp. 185-189.

12. D. Sauermann (ed.) *Weihnachten in Westfalen* (Münster in Westfalen 1976) p. 52.

13. Cf. A. Niederer in Foreword to R. Bautz *Zur Unrast der Jugend* (Frauenfeld-Stuttgart 1975) p. 5: 'Even though today's adolescents may be of much the same age as the young people who were formerly members of the *"Knabenschaften"*, there is an important difference between the two: those who belonged to the *"Knabenschaften"* were valued and treated as adults; as such they were concerned to preserve established social *mores* and their values were those of their parents' generation. Unlike many young people today, they were fully integrated into society.'

14. B. Grom 'Weihnachten feiern: Zwischen kritischem Engagement und neuem "Ja zum Feiern"' *Stimmen der Zeit* 101 (1976) p. 849.

15. *Ibid.*

16. M. Göpfert 'Der Glaube lebt von vertrauten Worten' *Orientierung* 41 (1977) pp. 127-130.

17. *Ibid.* The title of this section is 'Notwendigkeit religiöser Traditionsbildung'.

John Shea

A Theological Perspective on Human Relations Skills and Family Intimacy

'Oh, Mama, just look at me one minute as though you really saw me.'
Thornton Wilder, Our Town

(After two acts of plotted fratricides, adulteries, sibling rivalries, and family hatreds, the line is the mother's.) 'Well, what family doesn't have its ups and downs?'
James Goldman, The Lion in Winter

Since hidden agendas are out and surfaced assumptions are in, it is acceptable to be direct. This paper urges local churches to consider human relations skills training with an eye to family intimacy as essential ministerial activity. They should do this not because the psychological approach is relevant or because family life is often tumultuous and this might help or because the divorce rate is soaring and something must be done, but because the capacity for intimacy is a way of responding to the divine activity which permeates human life; and the Church, if it is to maintain its identity and vitality, must go with its God. To unpack this basic assertion four areas will be explored: (1) a working understanding of divine activity in human life, (2) the way in which the foundational Christian story focuses and develops this activity, (3) a conception of relational skills as the new ascesis, the way in which divine activity is responded to, and (4) the local church as the deliverer of divine-human relational skills.

DIVINE ACTIVITY IN HUMAN LIFE

All talk of divine activity in human life must be placed in the humbling context of Kurt Vonnegut's tale.

> I once knew an Episcopalian lady in Newport, Rhode Island, who asked me to design and build a doghouse for her Great Dane. The lady claimed to understand God and His Ways of Working perfectly. She could not understand why anyone should be puzzled about what had been or about what was going to be.
>
> And yet, when I showed her a blueprint of the doghouse I proposed to build, she said to me, 'I'm sorry, but I never could read one of those things'.
>
> 'Give it to your husband or your minister to pass on to God,' I said, 'and, when God finds a minute, I'm sure he'll explain this doghouse of mine in a way that even *you* can understand.'
>
> She fired me. I shall never forget her. She believed that God liked people in sailboats much better than He liked people in motorboats. She could not bear to look at a worm. When she saw a worm, she screamed.
>
> She was a fool, and so am I, and so is anyone who thinks he sees what God is Doing, [writes Bokonon].[1]

James Mackay points to the same caution with more theological precision.

> If one accepts the almost extreme agnosticism with regard to God's nature which Aquinas, for example, admits . . . why should one not accept at least an equal agnosticism with regard to God's actions? *Actio sequitur esse,* as the Scholastics used to say. More popularly put, the point would read: If the nature of a thing is known from its activity— and that is surely true in all cases—then it cannot be possible to claim to know more about the actions of something than one can know about its nature. Yet the very people who will admit that we know that God is but not what he is, immediately proceed to say with the utmost confidence that God acted with such intention at such a point in history or even in their own lives.[2]

The incomprehensibility of the God-Humankind relationship is the never-to-be forgotten context of all comprehensible statements.

A current emphasis in religious thinking is theological anthropology or anthropological theology. One implication of these phrases is that neither God nor humankind should be discussed independently. Divine and human reality so interpenetrate that any language about this co-reality must implicate both. To talk exclusively of God is to give the impression that this reality can be considered without taking into account its impact on human life. To talk exclusively of humankind is to give the impression that this reality can be adequately represented without taking into account the divine mystery which energises and supports it. Also to define the human without reference to the divine is to ensure imaginatively that the only way God will enter human life is by interruption and that the only way human life will touch God is by escaping its humanity. Theological anthropology attempts to focus on neither the realities of God nor humankind in themselves but on the relational flow between them.

This starting point—the mutual yet distinguishable interpenetration of God and humankind—restructures the religious imagination in two significant ways. First, the search for God is no longer construed as how to find the missing God but how to surface the ubiquitous God. Because God is present in and to human life there is no need to import him. In this imagination the former messengers of the unavailable God become the symbols of the available God. Dostoevski's phrase reflects this understanding: 'There is no such thing as a search for God for there is nothing in which He cannot be found.' Secondly, faith is changed from a belief in what cannot be seen to an interpretation of what cannot be escaped. The leap of faith is not guessing at the existence of a separate and absent reality but the risk of interpreting the intimate yet transcendent Mystery and living out of that interpretation.

This religious imagination, grounded in theological anthropology and with its distinctive understandings of God and faith, moves in two directions. First, it is sensitive to the transcendent Mystery in which humankind participates and, secondly, it formulates an understanding of the dynamic character of this encompassing Mystery. The awareness of a More, a Whole, a Presence is a sacramental.[3] In our interaction with other finite realities 'something more' than the finite realities involved enters awareness. Schillebeeckx calls this the transcendent Third which is present in all human experience and capable, at any given moment, of being disclosed. This awareness might be called the 'in and through' sensitivity which characterises much of contemporary theological writing.

> For at least the presence of God as the transcendental ground and horizon of everything which exists and everything which knows (and this is a presence of God, an immediacy to Him) takes place precisely *in and through* the presence of the finite existent.[4]
> We attain God only *in and through* the intramundane, of whose being he is the fountainhead.[5]

The first suggestion of this imagination is the oldest of humankind's instincts: we are not alone.

The second move of this imagination is toward an understanding of the transcendent Mystery as active and influential. It attempts to elaborate a working theory of the symbol 'God acts'. Although there are many models of divine activity,[6] one that seems particularly helpful for our purposes is the process model. The key factor in this model is that God's presence acts as a lure to the maximisation of beauty.[7] Beauty is distinctively understood as a quality of experience which holds in tension harmony and intensity. Every event, which in Whiteheadian terms, is a nexus of actual occasions, moves toward a gathering of all its elements into a positive synthesis. But this desire for harmony can be purchased at the price of intensity. When this occurs, the beauty is trivialised because the harmony is achieved at too low a level. The old example of this process is the dichotomous question: Would you prefer to dine with a pig or die with Socrates? Although the dinner with the pig may be harmonious, it is so trivial that the lure toward beauty might move you to share the intensity of Socrates' pain. The classic instance of the preference of intensity over harmony is Milton's Satan who would rather rule in hell than serve in heaven. But the question is not harmony or intensity but their continual interaction which is provoked by the divine presence in human life.

The need for intimacy, which seems built into the human developmental process, can be understood as an instance of the divine lure to beauty. Whatever else the experience of intimacy may be, it is certainly energised by the twin drives of harmony and intensity. An intimate relationship yearns to be a reconciled one, harmoniously integrating the persons involved. Yet this 'getting along' can turn deadly if the harmony is a surface achievement which has screened out depth feelings. In this situation the impulse to intimacy may lead toward intensity, living with the inevitable discord in the hope of a higher harmony. This understanding of intimacy allows for both intimate peace and intimate conflict. It embraces the full range of close relationships. Paramount to this understanding is the assumption that the human person is free to respond to this lure or neglect it, to actualise a high degree of beauty or be content with triviality.

Although no full phenomenology of intimacy will be attempted, a few remarks will help focus the general area. Thomas Oden's six ironies of intimate relationships concretely map the lure to intimate beauty.[8] His description centres on the dialectical relations of duration and ecstacy, accountability and negotiability, empathy and congruence, emotive warmth and conflict-capability, self-disclosure and letting-be, finitude and transcendence. Secondly, the word 'intimate' in popular usage often carries the connotation of genital sexual activity. Its use here is broader. Howard and Charlotte Clinebell have outlined twelve types of intimacy of which only one is sexual.[9] Further, this paper presumes that the initial and extremely important experiences of intimacy are familial. The family is the learning environment for interpersonal relations. If the relationships are healthy, the capacity for beauty is heightened. The ongoing familial task could be described as the transformation of physical proximity into intimate closeness.

If God is present in human life as the lure to beauty and one significant locus of this lure is the urge to intimate relationships, the natural question is: How do we respond, how do we follow the lure? But before engaging that question, the Christian story must be consulted to enrich our understanding.

THE CHRISTIAN STORY AND INTIMACY

Every people, if they are truly a people, have a collection of touchstone stories. These are stories that belong to the people as a whole and are considered to have a special claim on reality. These stories are continually consulted as this people journey through life. Individual biographies are interwoven with the special stories and out of the dialogue come convictions, attitudes, and behaviour. Although the stories may be written down in a book, they only really happen in the mouths of people. The book does not exist on its own but belongs to the people who carry and read it. It is the story off the page and into the mind and heart that counts. In this sense touchstone stories are never slavishly repeated but always creatively retold to bring about new understandings and action. They are the same yet ever changing for new people tell them and they are received in new situations.

Christian touchstone stories concern God. Yet from our basic positioning in theological anthropology this means that they perceive the human situation from the ultimate and imperative perspective of divine presence. Therefore to tell a touchstone story of God is to focus initially on the general area of human life where divine presence and activity has been experienced and, consequently, to develop the meanings which this activity suggests. This dynamic, how stories function religiously for the people who tell them, needs to be fully understood before the story of the Loving God which focuses on intimate relationships can be told.

The initial starting point is the actual experience in which the presence and activity of God was brought to consciousness. For example, in my experience of interpersonal love I become aware of a transpersonal source, a true otherness, which legitimates and encourages my feelings and behaviours. Therefore, to focus this elusive Presence I linguistically 'separate it out' and name it with the feelings, attitudes, and values through which it entered awareness, e.g., God is love. But this initial metaphoric activity which points to the experience of love as the locus of the divine cannot convey the full 'weight' of the experience. So the experience through this initial metaphor of love provokes a story which will more adequately explore it. God's love is elaborated in tales of His personal knowledge and fidelity, His entry into human life (incarnation), His sharing of our pain (crucifixion), etc. But the Christian people not only tell stories which relate them to reality, they mine the wisdom of those stories in systematic thought. In this way Christian theologies of love are developed. The Christian storytelling process is a complex enterprise which entails experience, metaphor, story, and wisdom.

Three features of this storytelling process are significant. First, it is symbolic. The metaphor, story, and wisdom are not meant to have a life of their own. They are not substitutes for the experience but ways of returning to the area of human life which generated the metaphor, story, and wisdom and entering it through their developed meanings. With the suggestion of T. S. Eliot the process is one of exploration and return.

> We shall not cease from exploration
> And the end of all our exploring
> Will be to arrive where we started
> And know the place for the first time.

Language is functioning symbolically when it carries the speaker and hearer into the experience.

Secondly, this process is artistic. It is a creative telling which respects past meanings but does not hesitate to transform them out of its own inspiration. For example, on the level of historical interest the Christian people investigate the understandings of divine love in the Book of Hosea and the Gospel of John and note similarities and differences. However, in the process of storytelling they will mix and match and develop the themes in an interlocking way out of the impulses that are generated by the present experience. The theological rationale for this freedom is that the same spirit who urged the original creation of the stories animates us today. Therefore, the stories are as malleable as the spirit and the people who co-authored them. They are not unchanging deposits but ongoing tales to which each generation supplies fresh content. They are only finished when the last Christian is silent.

This notion of a continually constructed story is obviously a risky business. The best check against excess, and the third feature of the storytelling process, is its communal base. The stories are always retold by the people and their meanings worked out not in isolation, not even the isolation of the solitary genius, but in the company of believers. In other words, the Church is the key hermeneutical principle. This community context of the storytelling process means that stories belong to no one person but to the entire people.

With this understanding of religious storytelling as a context, contemporary Christians engaged in the struggles of intimate living *might* remember and retell their touchstone story of the Loving God in this way. The Lord of All There Is personally knows us. He knows us through and through. 'You know when I sit and when I stand; even before a word is on my tongue, behold O Lord, you know the whole of it.' Even when we become afraid and flee such a searching presence, this loving God pursues us. 'If I go to the heavens, you are there; if I sink to the nether world, you are present there.' The bond of this God's knowledge and love is the most powerful of all realities. 'For I am certain that neither death nor life, neither angels nor principalities, neither the present nor the future, nor powers, neither height nor depth nor any other creature, will be able to separate us from the love of God that comes to us in Christ Jesus our Lord.' Our God is a faithful lover.

The overwhelming love of God urges him to be with us. The epistle to the Philippians says that he did not 'cling' to his divinity but poured himself into flesh.

> But God's own descent
> Into flesh was meant
> As a demonstration
> That the supreme merit
> Lay in risking spirit
> In substantiation.[10]

The incarnation is God's empathic entry into our lives. His reason, like that of all lovers, is that he desired union with his beloved. But this union was not overpowering, absorbing us into his reality. God's union with us, his sharing of our lives, is empowering. Irenaeus spoke it sharply, 'The glory of God is man fully alive'. God's empathic sharing of our lives did not back off diminishment. He suffered and died on a cross so that suffering and death would not be solitary and anxious. His faithful presence to us is both a gift and a challenge, ever supporting us and ever opening us to the new.

All Christians who hear this skeletal story will add and question it, and each addition and question will be a revelation of who we are and who the God is who journeys with us. Others may mention covenant and forgiveness, talk of resistance and fear, distinguish agape and eros. But all are telling, in ever greater nuance and richness, the ongoing Christian story of the Loving God. Now stories such as this, when told by the Christian peoples, direct attention to personal, intimate relationships as the locus of the divine activity. They also suggest some elements of the divine lure in these situations—fidelity, personal knowledge, empathy, union, sacrifice, etc. From these suggestions a Christian wisdom about love is developed.

In summary: there is present to all human life a divine activity which lures us to beauty. One area where this lure to harmony and intensity is present is intimate family relationships. Christians direct attention and elaborate the meaning of this activity by creatively re-telling their touchstone stories. This complex storytelling process latches onto the elusive divine presence and, if it is working well, the speechless God once again becomes Word. In the story of the Loving God the lure to loving, intimate relationships is focused. The question becomes: How do we respond to the lure?

DIVINE-HUMAN RELATIONS SKILLS

Human relations skills only increase the probability of effective relating. They are not magical techniques for deteriorating family relationships or insurance against strife and upset. The underlying assumption (one that is only partially valid) is that if people understand the dynamics of human relating in general and their own style in particular and are skilled in acting out of that understanding, the chances for enriching intimate relationships are better. Human relations skills are ways people own and direct their lives in the interpersonal sphere.

But from the faith perspective sketched in the first two sections they are also responses to the divine lure for intimate beauty implanted in human life and revealed in the Christian story of the Loving God. Therefore, their proper designation would be divine-human relations skills because they answer both human and divine calls. Skills are a contemporary ascesis, a highly disciplined yet artful (non-mechanistic) shaping of the divine-human world. They function precisely as the more traditional practises of prayer and fasting. They are ways of contacting and responding to the divine presence. But the emphasis appears different because in this understanding the divine impulse is conjoined and manifested in the interpersonal drive. Therefore, the pursuit of God is not an individual, independent effort at sanctity but a way of belonging to another person guided by the convictions and values of the Christian stories.

At this juncture religious thinking often moves the discussion away from the development of skills. It prefers to direct attention to an ambivalence in the drive for intimacy. It points to a contradictory strain, an inner resistance, a core of fear which continually undercuts all efforts at intimacy. We covertly subvert what we overtly desire. The predicament is not lack of skills or ignorance or external circumstances but a fundamental disorientation within the person himself. This analysis convicts humankind of a self-preoccupation so total and debilitating that no effort can overcome it. The solution cannot arise from the problem, so we must look beyond ourselves for salvation. The path is cleared for the advent of Christ who meets our recognition of total need with His offer of total grace.

Although this understanding focuses both on how embedded and determining our fears are and on how intimate relationships usually have a quality of gift (grace) about them, it tends to overlook the commonsense wisdom that for relationships to be healthy, you have to work at them. It might be fruitful (if not totally adequate) to approach the question from the perspective that intimate human relationships often fail or are not sustained on any meaningful level because people just do not know how to do it. This is not to say that there are no dark urges toward self-betrayal but that a significant factor in that betrayal is the fear of relating well and so the ensuing self-preoccupation. Skilled and effective relating increases the probability that the hesitancy at the centre can be creatively countered—not by human effort alone but by human response to divine lure. In other words, from the imagination of anthropological theology, the solution arises from the people and the God who have the problem.

A second reaction to skills training for interpersonal living (this time from the secular, not the religious, side) is that it is out of place. The interpersonal sphere, it is believed, should be spontaneous and natural. Skills give the impression of manipulation and calculated response. But human relations skills are not rigid procedures which, if followed, produce intimacy. They are sensitivities which enable flexibility and depth in human relating. It is true that there is nothing more killing to intimacy than skills used without art. They become monotonous techniques divorced from their life-giving source in the uniqueness of the person. But when they are integrated into a personal style, they become ways of being fully present to other people.

The Christian story of the loving God suggests three sets of skills— self-disclosure, empathic, and challenging.[11] The ability to be in touch with your own feelings and to be able to communicate those feelings concretely and accurately is an initial step in interpersonal living. Not to be able to discern personal feelings is to be their prisoner: not to be able to communicate them is to remain alone. The Loving God did not think it a good thing to 'cling' to his lofty isolation but revealed himself so that we might know him. Empathy is the ability to enter and participate in the thought and feeling world of another. In order to do this listening and responding skills are necessary. To merely say 'I understand' is seldom enough. The Loving God entered into our world, understood the panic of the running heart, and took on estrangement and death. Challenging skills point to the need in human relationships to hear and speak other perspectives. This is perhaps the most crucial and most difficult skill. How to confront so that confrontation leads to growth and renewed closeness rather than paralysis and further distance is a skill always in need of development. In the Christian story the Loving God convicts us of non-love in such a way that we are empowered and not enervated. These sets of skills, although not totally covering the interpersonal sphere, are foundational to any healthy relationship. The concepts behind the skills are relatively simple. The actual ability is relatively difficult.

THE LOCAL CHURCH AS DELIVERER OF DIVINE-HUMAN RELATIONS SKILLS

For lack of a more eloquent definition—the Church is that group which hangs around the divine activity in human life as revealed and interpreted through the event of Jesus the Christ. Ministers are those people within this larger group who point to, talk about, facilitate, encourage, direct, and otherwise help the larger group to celebrate this divine activity. If this is the case, Christian ministry should consider skills training for effective human relating a 'fitting' task. Skills are a concrete way of responding to the concrete God.

There is an old story worth retelling. There was a village of caring people located downstream on a river. One day bodies began floating down the river. The villagers fished them out. Some were alive; some were dead. The dead they properly buried. The live ones they rushed to hospitals and cared for them. Every day new bodies appeared and every day the villagers went about their saving chores. Soon the ones who survived married, and homes and schools had to be built. The village quickly tripled its size and new problems of crime and pollution appeared. And every day the bodies came down the river. The villagers prided themselves on their solicitude for their neighbour in need and never shirked their duty. But no one went to the top of the river to find out why the bodies were floating down.

To be a minister to family life in a local church is often to be in a downstream position. The interpersonal casualties are coming down and all time and effort is spent in family counselling. What becomes obvious is that people have not had the opportunity to develop the skills they need to live with each other. Skills training is an upstream approach. It looks at the possible causes of (1) chronic family discord, (2) tepid, non-family co-existence in the same house, and (3) normal family problems. It suggests that people skilled in interpersonal living will more effectively enter into the demanding and rewarding experience of being a family. In this wide sense skills training might be characterised as preventive ministry.

It is too grandiose, but also irresistible, to mention Nietzsche's remark that the man who has a powerful enough 'why' to live can endure almost any 'how'. This paper does not consider *how* skills training can be incorporated into local church ministry. It merely states the *why* with the hope that if the *why* is powerful enough, the *how* will be pursued.

Notes

1. K. Vonnegut, Jr. *Cat's Cradle* (New York 1963) p. 13.

2. D. Mackay *The Problems of Religious Faith* (Chicago 1972) pp. 183-84.

3. For a fuller understanding of this approach see J. Shea *The Stories of God* (Chicago 1978) chap. 1.

4. K. Rahner *Foundations of Christian Faith* (New York 1978) p. 83.

5. E. Schillebeeckx *God and Man* (New York 1969) p. 164.

6. Consult I. G. Barbour *Myths, Models and Paradigms* (New York 1974) pp. 155-70.

7. For a fuller understanding consult J. B. Cobb, Jr. *A Christian Natural Theology* (Philadelphia 1965) pp. 92-135.

8. T. Oden *Game Free* (New York 1974) pp. 2-25.

9. H. J. Clinebell Jr. and C. H. Clinebell *The Intimate Marriage* (New York 1970).

10. R. Frost *The Poetry of Robert Frost* (New York 1969).

11. For a fuller understanding of the skills approach to human relating and training methods available consult G. Egan *Interpersonal Living* (Monterey, Ca. 1976) and *The Skilled Helper* (Monterey, Ca. 1975).

David Tracy

The Catholic Model of Caritas: Self-transcendence and Transformation

1. SOME GENERAL DEFINITIONS

IN THE theological literature, Catholic and Protestant, there are some standard terms which are employed. Since I use these terms throughout this paper, it may prove helpful to provide some initial definitions of the terms at the beginning. The attached syllabi provide the basic bibliographical information for theology. The secondary materials (especially Outka) also provide further resources (e.g., D'Arcy, von Balthasar) worth noting. The definitions (which are my own reformulations from the literature) are:

Agape—the gift of God's love in Jesus Christ: it is given; not our achievement—but pure gift, sheer grace which enobles, empowers, elicits Christians to love God and neighbour in the self-sacrificial manner that God has first loved us in Jesus Christ.

Eros—human striving, yearning of a self for some ideal of happiness as concretely experienced in all concrete human loves; classically expressed in Plato; reformulated in almost every age in accordance with some reigning paradigm in what constitutes authentic human love.

Libido—the pure desire aspect of *eros* abstracted from the self's conscious ideal of happiness. Since Freud, often identified with powerful sexual drive.

Philia—friendship-love; the love of the other as related to the self and the self's own desires, attachments, ideals—(related to but not necessarily identical with neighbour-love).

Caritas (Charity)—Since Augustine, the reigning Catholic model: a proposal for a *synthesis* of human *eros* in the self and the divine *agape* given in Jesus Christ. The particular understandings of both *eros* and *agape* change from one Catholic theologian to another. In every case, however—as this paper shall argue—some synthesis will be formulated; more exactly some transformation of human *eros* (which is basically affirmed) by divine *agape* will be explicated to disclose the concrete and complex experiential reality of *caritas* in Christian lives.

Nomos—love's expression through a fulfilment of law. Often (mistakenly) thought by Christians to represent Judaism's notion of love; genuinely representative, however, of any purely legalistic understanding of either Judaism or Christianity.

It is important to note that these definitions represent my own attempts to achieve a relative consensus on factors debated in the literature. Each definition, for example, is self-consciously distinct from the famous definitions (especially of *agape* and *eros*) delineated by Anders Nygren in his ground-breaking work *Agape and Eros*.

2. THEOLOGY AND THE TASK OF CORRELATION
ON THE REALITY OF CHRISTIAN LOVE

In general terms, Christian theology is a discipline which attempts to correlate the meaning and truth of the Christian fact (its scriptures, doctrines, rituals, witnesses, symbols, etc.) with the meaning and truth of our contemporary experience. When the theologian is principally engaged in one of the three major disciplines within theology (viz. fundamental, systematic, and practical theologies), this fact ordinarily influences the *emphasis* which either side of the correlation will receive. However, every theologian will in fact be involved in some form of correlation of these two realities.

The more explicit form of a model for that procedure of correlation can take several forms. The strictly logical possibilities for correlation can map the three major models actually employed in the history of Christian theology. The most basic logical differences are those among three options: 'all', 'some' and 'none'. In theological models these logical options for correlating Christian and secular experience become models of identity (all), confrontation (none) and transformation (some).

1. *Confrontation*: This position holds that there is *no* correlation between our ordinary human loves (friendship, romantic love; various forms of intimacy, etc.) and the divine love given to us in Jesus Christ. This model is more exactly described as a model of *confrontation* between

our ordinary experience and the pure gift of God's revelation. In more general terms, this option is expressed clearly in the famous rhetorical question of Tertullian, 'What has Athens to do with Jerusalem?' On the question of love, it is most clearly expressed in Nygren's interpretation of Luther and Paul whereby only the gift of *agape* is Christian love. That gift must *never* be confused with, synthesised with, or even really correlated with the various forms of human striving which constitute eros-love in all its modalities. The correlation is paradoxically that there is *no* correlation between *agape* and any form of *eros*; a refusal to face that confrontational reality is, on this reading, a betrayal of the Christian understanding of *agape* love by reducing it to some reigning form of *eros* love.

2. *Identity*: This position holds that there is a complete correlation between Christian agapic love and the love of *eros* in our ordinary experiences of friendship, love, and intimacy. This model for correlation is really one of identity. Ultimately the pure giftedness of any love is identical to the gift of God's love for us in Jesus Christ. Appeals to our common human experiences of intimacy, therefore, would suffice for understanding Christian love. There is ordinarily little recognition of, or, at least, little accounting for, the actual ambiguity in our human experience of intimacy. Rather the purely positive sides of that experience are highlighted (the creativity, ecstasy, loyalty, and fundamental trust present in all authentic human experiences of love). The 'negative' aspects of that experience (the self-aggrandisement, the delusions, the angers and jealousies, the fears and insecurities) are ordinarily either ignored or at least downplayed. Hence Christian love is no more, and no less, than a clearer, a more explicit consciousness of the common human experience of the giftedness, creativity and fundamental trust present in our everyday positive experiences of intimacy and love.

3. *Transformation*: Most theologians develop some explicitly transformation model for understanding the correlations between the gift of love in Jesus Christ and our common experience of love. Most contemporary Christian theologians, Catholic and Protestant, in fact employ some particular model of correlation. Indeed the mainline Catholic theological understanding of the relationships between faith and reason, theology and philosophy, *agape* and *eros* encourages many theologians to believe that the transformation model of correlation is, in fact, the major model for historical and contemporary Catholic theology. On the question of a theological understanding of love, for example, there seems no doubt that the *caritas* tradition present in Catholic Christianity from Augustine to our own day is *the* paradigm worthy of our communal reflection. Indeed, even before Augustine named 'Caritas' this attempted synthesis of the pure giftedness of God's agapic love in Jesus Christ with the individual's search for happiness in the legitimate and necessary

strivings of authentic eros-love, the reality of correlation was present in the Christian tradition. Synthesis was clearly present in the *Logos* theologies of the East: witness Gregory of Nyssa's mystical theology of *eros* and *agape*. The reality of a correlation possibility of synthesis, moreover, is present, in my judgment, in the New Testament itself. Indeed, as Nygren himself admits, it may be found in at least implicit form in the Johannine tradition. Many recent scriptural studies have shown how its presence may be seen in both the synoptics (including—indeed, for myself, especially—in the parables of Jesus) as well as in the insistence of Paul that Christian love is both gift and command, that Christian love both challenges and fulfils all authentic striving.

In a similar manner, the New Testament challenges any easy identity of Christian love and the 'loves' of our common human experience. Indeed God's love for us in Christ Jesus and in the covenant with Israel is always thought of as *pure gift,* as *grace* which enables, empowers, frees us to love as God has first loved us in Christ Jesus. The pure gift character of authentic Christian love and, in that properly theological sense, the purely *agapic* graced character of that love is the clear and consistent witness of the entire Christian tradition from the scriptures to the present. Any implicit or explicit *identity* model for the relationships between that love and our common human experience of love must, therefore, show how that common witness can be ignored or retranslated into that alternative of identity (on purely hermeneutical grounds). I do not myself see any way by which an identity model could really account for the pure giftedness, the event-happening-grace character of love present in the authentic Christian tradition.

This latter judgment seems even more secure when one recognises the 'extreme' human possibilities of love which the New Testament commands: the love of the enemy; that radical self-sacrificial love decisively represented in the love of the Cross of Christ; the love of every and each neighbour precisely as neighbour (not merely as 'friend'). Each of these commands are 'extreme' or extraordinary commands; it is *recognised* that they do not accord with our *ordinary* experience of love, fidelity, intimacy, friendship. Indeed, there is profound truth in Friedrich Nietzsche's insistence that New Testament Christianity was, in fact, a revaluation of all ancient values. This is the case precisely because, by its insistence upon real neighbour love—even the love of the enemy and the self-sacrifice of the Cross—Christianity challenged the then reigning paradigm for love, the 'friendship' paradigm of the ancient Greeks. Neighbour-love is a command for the Christian, indeed a command to a life at the limits. Yet that command is never simply command because in Christian self-understanding, the Christian is enobled, empowered, gifted, graced to hear and fulfil that command. Do these scriptural reflections then mean, in effect, that only a confrontation model between Christian *agape* and human *eros* will suffice? As indicated above, a pure confrontation model is itself challenged by both scripture and by the mainline Christian witness—certainly by the Catholic *caritas* model for love. It is necessary, therefore, to provide some further reflections upon the character of a theological transformation model.

It worth recalling that in the Catholic theological tradition, there are, in fact, no real major exceptions to the tradition's rejection of both a pure identity and a pure confrontation model. Rather every major Catholic theologian, when reflecting on the reality of love within the Catholic experience, works out a particular transformation model whereby both *agape* and *eros* are correlated into the classical Catholic synthesis of *caritas*. Moreover, there is no doubt that the Catholic *caritas* position on love is not an exception unrelated to other major choices in Catholic theology: a trust in reason along with a religious recognition of the pure giftedness of faith informing various Catholic formulations of the relationships between 'faith' and 'reason'; a profound religious conviction of the radicality and universality of God's grace informing the classical dictum that grace fulfills but does not destroy nature (including, therefore, *eros*); an anthropology which, while cognisant of the reality of sin in the human condition, tends to emphasise the transformation even of sin by the power of God's grace; Catholic anthropology thereby develops a vision of our common humanity which seems both realistic (on the genuine ambiguity of all human actions) yet optimistic on the alternate triumph of grace in the human spirit and in history. With Albert Camus, the authentic Catholic sensibility ordinarily belives that 'There is more in human beings to admire than to despise.' That same sensibility develops an analogical imagination which attempts to order the relationships of God and humankind, nature and history, justice and love, *agape* and *eros* by means of the transformative focal meaning of God's grace in Christ Jesus.

There are almost always major exceptions in the Catholic tradition to at least one of the positions summarised above. The 'later' Augustine and Pascal, for example, are, in fact, less optimistic about the human situation than most Catholic theologians and thereby tend to relate grace to sin more than to nature. And yet even in Augustine and Pascal the final triumph of grace resounds and the caritas-synthesis is clearly affirmed. Indeed from Augustine through Bernard, Aquinas, Bonaventure, Dante, Pascal, and Newman to D'Arcy, Schler, von Balthasar, Rahner, Lonergan and Kung, the same *leitmotiv* recurs with different resonances and distinct formulations for the exact character of the transformation: Christian love is best understood on the synthetic and tranformative model of *caritas*. Both *agape* and *eros* are to be affirmed and correlated into some higher synthesis to redescribe the human situation and to prescribe those dispositions, habits, and character which are properly 'loving'.

The exact nature of the correlation of *agape* and *eros* will shift from age to age and even from theologian to theologian in accordance with particular interpretations of both New Testament *agape* and a major contemporary model of *eros*. For example, the individual theologian's 'canon within the canon' for understanding New Testament *agape* is, for example, the radically self-sacrificial Kenotic model of Paul's theology of the Cross. Or that canon may be a Johannine incarnational model which emphasises the 'mutuality' factor in love and the cosmic reality of God's descending love in the *Logos* and human ascending love in the Christian community. Still other theologians may well turn to the parables or the various formulations of the Great Command in the Synoptics to find their major paradigm for love. Then one may well find an emphasis upon the reality of love as both pure gift (in the parables) *and* radical command (to love God and neighbour). And yet however central a particular paradigm for New Testament love may prove ('self-sacrifice', 'mutuality', 'love for God', 'love of the neighbour'—often reformualted as 'radical equal regard'), no reader of the New Testament can fail to note that authentic love is presented as both pure gift and radical command. Catholic interpreters will ordinarily also note that *agape* does not merely displace or destroy *eros* but—as in the incarnational and sacramental vision of John—transforms all *eros* into genuine *caritas*.

The exact nature of the model of transformation will also depend upon the particular (ordinarily the cultural) model for authentic *eros* which the theologian employs to understand the authentic *eros* love of our ordinary experience. One may employ (as did Gregory of Nyssa) a neo-Platonic model with its metaphor of the purification of *eros* as one ascends 'the ladder of love' lesser loves to the reality of 'spiritual' *eros*—love for the Loving God. One may employ (as did Thomas Aquinas) an Aristotelian model of authentic friendship to understand both our relationships to one another and to God. One may employ a model of courtly love, or romantic love, or some modern psychological model (Freud, Jung, Erikson, Fromm *et al*.) to understand the *eros* of our cultural experience. For example, we as a group are anxious to understand the realities of 'intimacy' among contemporary persons as our reigning and best authentic *eros* model for loving actions and attitudes among human beings. There is always present some model of what the classical writers named 'eros' to understand the reality of love in our lives—with all its giftedness, ecstacies, creativity *and* ambiguity. Hence, contemporary Catholics, either implicitly or explicitly, attempt to understand and make their contributions from *their* cultural experience to the *caritas* synthesis of Catholic Christianity. By way of some initial and tentative suggestions along these same lines, I will close this brief essay with a discussion of a model of theological transformation as related to certain contemporary models of *eros*.

3. TRANSFORMATION AND CONTEMPORARY SELF-TRANSCENDENCE

From a Christian theological viewpoint, love may be recognised as the concrete experiential form of grace. For grace is the Christian theological word for describing the event, happening, gift of God's self-communication in creation and redemption. On the experiential side, the reality of grace is experienced in the pure giftedness of life itself and in the gift-experiences of the explicitly 'theological virtues': faith, hope, and love. The reality of the giftedness of life can and is experienced in such positive 'limit-experiences' as a heightened consciousness of creativity, a fundamental trust in the very meaningfulness of our existence despite all threats, an abiding joy and a sense of life-enhancing joy in loyalty to an authentic cause of justice. The same experienced reality of pure giftedness is felt in the self-transcending power and force of all authentic human love: love of a tradition, a nation, a church, a cause above all, love of persons—friends, family, 'the neighbour' and God. The intensity of these experiences of love can range from the more ordinary experiences of our everyday sense of trust, creativity, and loyalty to those intensifications of these experiences of faith, hope, love which we call mystical states of consciousness.

For the Christian, all these experiences named not merely the gift, event, happening of the self's transcendence of its usual and often fairly lack-lustre consciousness but sheer grace, the experienced reality of God's self-communication to us in Jesus Christ. For the decisive communication, manifestation, revelation of that radical grace is, for the Christian, precisely God's manifestation of both who we are and who God is in Jesus Christ. In Christ—and thereby in the word and sacrament of Christ's Church—we know and name this common human experience of pure gift, 'grace'. We know and say—in facing and allowing the reality of that gift into our conscious experience—that reality itself, despite all indications to the contrary, is finally gracious; that the final reality with which we all must deal is neither our own pathetic attempts at self-salvation, nor the tragedy of life in all its masks, nor even the frightening reality of sin in our constant attempts to delude ourselves and others, but rather the hard, unyielding reality of the Pure Unbounded Love disclosed to us in God's revelation of who God is and who we too finally are in Christ Jesus.

Grace, therefore, is that gift; it is most clearly experienced in what Christians name radical faith, authentic hope and agapic love. As pure gift it transforms our ordinary experience in three principal ways. First, it displaces 'our hearts of stone with hearts of flesh'. It displaces our constant temptation to trap ourselves within the self, to refuse to let go of the self *'curvatus in se'*, to refuse to believe, or hope, that we need not justify ourselves to God, to others, or to ourselves. Rather that radical forgiveness and acceptance is already given, to us as the pure justifying grace of Jesus Christ.

Yet as the Catholic tradition has insisted, this crucial radical displacement process is neither the final nor the grounding reality of the transformative power of grace. We experience the displacement of our sin *because* we experience God's replacement of all our strivings—with the pure gift of that grace. When that experience is really allowed full sway in the self, we may recognise both the empowering and enobling reality of radical Christian self-sacrificial love (as in those best moments of our lives for one another; as, paradigmatically, in those we name 'saints' and 'witnesses'; as decisively in the Cross of Jesus Christ). We may also recognise the empowering and evocative experience of 'mutal love' (as in those experiences of authentic community, real friendship and intimacy, real trust in and loyalty to this person, this group, this community, this cause). When that experience is more muted, for whatever conscious or unconscious reasons, then, I believe, we must face and recognise the reality of the *command* to love God and neighbour. In experiences of true friendship, in authentic community, in real mutuality and self-sacrifice, we need not focus upon that command. For in those moments we actually experience—whether we name it so or not is here relatively secondary—the pure gift of God's grace in *the* gift of authentic, self-transcending love. At other times we must listen to the command to love: the stranger, the broken community, the frightening God of our frightened selves, even, let us recall, the enemy: that command must come in such moments to the forefront of our consciousness. For the command is itself gift: we are commanded because we are enobled and empowered; we can displace our frenzied attempts to justify and accept ourselves and others because we have already been justified and accepted in Jesus Christ; we can displace the self from first place of attention because that self has already been replaced by the gift of God's *agapic* love and the freedom it gives in listening to and attempting to respond to the command to love.

And yet, in the Catholic tradition, this replacement-displacement movement of transformation must not be thought of in a merely extrinsic manner (as in some doctrines of 'forensic justification'). For the self is not radically evil, utterly corrupt, hopelessly fallen. Rather that self, in the Catholic view, is wounded but not—short of an implausible complete turn to radical evil—utterly corrupt. All the strivings of the self, in sum, are not necessarily selfish. All self-interest is not mere self-aggrandisement. Rather the fidelity of the self in its striving for, yearning for, working for a better self, a purer love (its *eros*)—all this is not to be rejected as utter corruption, pure 'works-righteousness'. All authentic *eros* love—the yearning of the human heart for authentic happiness as Augustine named it; the natural desire of our minds and hearts to see God, as Aquinas called it—is itself affirmed, transformed and converted by God's *agape*.

The displacement-replacement process of transformation by God's grace in Jesus Christ both restores our weakened and wounded but *real* capacity for authentic *eros* and fulfills that constant, driving, powerful force of *eros* love in all its forms. For *agape* discloses the reality of who God is: Pure Unbounded Love, and who we in fact are: graced, gifted, accepted persons loved by the God of Jesus Christ; and enobled, empowered, commanded to love each and all in turn. The continuing transformation of all our *eros* love by God's *agape* is what *caritas* finally is; *caritas* assumes that the strivings of *eros* are neither irrelevant nor evil in relationship to the gift of *agape*. More specifically, as Aquinas recognised, it is not irrelevant for the Christian to turn to the Aristotelian model of authentic friendship *and* not to reject it as 'pagan', 'corrupt', 'selfish', but to transform it in the light of God's self-revelation in the *agape* of Jesus Christ. In an age when Aristotle's model of friendship, Plato's model of the ascending ladder of *eros,* or Dante's model of courtly love are unlikely to present the major model for a contemporary self-understanding of the *eros*-tradition, then it is plausible and warranted for Christians to try to formulate a distinctly modern *eros* model in keeping with modern notions of authentic 'intimacy'. Thereby we may be able to understand *eros* as we in fact experience it. If we focus upon that model (or models) of authentic intimacy as experienced in our world, as understood by the disciplines present in our post-classical culture, as related to the classical models for *eros*-love present in the long and rich Catholic tradition, then one may hope that modern understandings of intimacy may themselves be transformed into some new and disclosive *caritas* synthesis which speaks to us and our contemporaries with the same power and truth that Augustine, Aquinas and Dante could speak to and for their age.

Indeed, if one looks at our own culture we can, I believe, find analogues to the theological models of identity, confrontation, and transformation which I have outlined above. The secular analogue of the theological identity-model is the model of pure self-fulfilment widespread in American culture. What have been named by cultural anthropologists 'cultures of joy' find ready acceptance in many aspects of the contemporary demand for genuine self-fulfilment. Nor is there any good theological reason for a tradition accepting a *caritas* model to reject the drive to self-fulfilment out of hand. Joy, creativity, ecstasy (a fulfilled self) are, after all, legitimate and enriching desires of the human spirit. Yet if *only* self-fulfilment is one's model for the self, then the route to the 'New Narcissism', or the route, more radically stated, to the self *'curvatus in se'* seems all to close at hand.

The secular analogue of the confrontative model may be found in various models for a 'culture of control'. Indeed so frightened can some secular critics of our culture's seeming obsession with self-fulfilment become that a whole spectrum of positions (ranging from the chastened liberalism of the Freudian critic, Philip Rieff, to various forms of neo-conservatism) has emerged to demand some new and secular form of a 'culture of control'. The demands for the recognition in any society which is also a civilisation of the need for self-discipline, (even) for a repression of some demands for self-fulfilment in the light of the common good—in a word for some reasonable control—are as clearly needed by our culture as for any prior one. Indeed Freud himself well matched the pessimism of the later Augustine in his insisting upon discipline, even repression, to allow 'civilisation'. A tradition which recognises the reality of sin, the ambiguity of all our actions, the need for disciplined reflection and discernment in the stages of the spiritual life—in short, the Catholic theological tradition—should not hesitate to incorporate these legitimate criticisms into a Catholic vision of *caritas*. Yet just as the 'cultures of joy' can too easily become 'the new narcissism', so too the 'culture of control' model may all too easily become a mere 'return of the repressed, the resentful, the weak'.

The most relatively adequate secular analogue to *caritas*-transformation, I believe, may be found in what might be named models of self-transcendence. In a manner analogous to the transformation demands recognising both intellectual complexity, and existential ambiguity, the model of self-transcendence sublates the genuine demands of both self-fulfilment and self-discipline. For self-transcendence preserves the reality of the self's drive to authentic fulfilment and the self's need for real discipline; it challenges and corrects the temptations of the first to narcissism and of the second to weak *ressentiment*; it sublates or transforms both into a model wherein the self's very fulfilment and most needed discipline may be found in the reality of authentic, consistent and lasting self-transcendence.

It is no mere accident that in contemporary theology most major Christian theologians employ some model of transformation allied with some secular paradigm of self-transcendence. In contemporary Catholic theology, for example, both Bernard Lonergan and Karl Rahner have developed particular models of both transformation and self-transcendence.

When Lonergan, for example, appeals to the need for intellectual, moral and religious 'conversion' for theologians, he means that the realities of cognitive, moral and religious self-transcendence must be acknowledged. For in cognitive self-transcendence the authentic self transcends its own needs, fears, desires in critical and rigorous intellectual inquiry determined to discover what is the case, not what I would like to be the case. That same self may also move past the desires of mere satisfaction and the fears of resentment into a world of authentic values and enduring character in moral self-transcendence. That same self may find and respond to the gift of God's love 'flooding our hearts' (Romans 5:5) and freeing us to become lovers of God and neighbour—in an unrestricted fashion in religious self-transcendence. Note here how the *eros* of inquiry, the call to true value are sublated (preserved, yet surpassed) in the higher synthesis of the agapic and erotic love of *caritas*. The authentic strivings and demands of every self for self-fulfilment (for what the classical writers called happiness) are respected and enhanced. The authentic need for discipline at every stage (in intellectual, moral and spiritual struggle) is respected and enhanced. Yet all are sublated into a model of self-transcendence which represents, I believe, the clearest contemporary expression of the Catholic *caritas* synthesis.

The synthetic model of *caritas*—and its recognition of *eros* and *agape,* gift and command, self-transcendence and transformation—may, I believe, serve as an appropriate Catholic theological model for reflection upon modern understandings of human intimacy. Yet to state the model is to state an ideal form for consideration, not an actualised reality; the hard work of refining, correcting, expanding, indeed of realising the new form which the *caritas* synthesis might take for our culture and our age is at hand. And that is a task which only the communal efforts of our several disciplines and our several envisionments of reality might yet allow.

Bibliography

Aristotle *Nicomachean Ethics* (Shields-Matges)
Burnaby, J. *Amor in St Augustine*
Furnish, V. *The Love Command in the New Testament*
Kegley, C. W., (ed.) *The Philosophy and Theology of Anders Nygren*
Luther, M. *Commentary on Romans*
Luther, M. *Freedom of the Christian*
Luther, M. *Lectures on Galatians* (Pelican edition, Vol. 26)
Nygren, A. *Agape and Eros* Introduction and Part 1 (Pargerl-Rike)
Nygren, A. *On the Soul and Resurrection*
Plato *Symposium* (Harrington-Starter)
Snaith, N. H. *Distinctive Ideas of the Old Testament* (Keifeit & Columbo)

Contributors

MARY DURKIN was born in Chicago, Illinois, in 1934. She is an associate professor in Religious Studies and Director of the Office of Moral and Religious Education at the University of Dayton, Ohio. She has written articles on marriage and the family, and has published *The Suburban Woman: Her Changing Role In The Church* (1975).

JACQUES GRAND'MAISON was born in 1944 at Saint-Jérome, Canada. He has carried out research into the family in Chicago and elsewhere, especially in Italy, Belgium and France. He has been professor at Montreal University since 1965 and he has published a large number of books and shorter studies, the latest of which are *Une philosophie de la vie* (1977), *Une société en quête d'éthique* (1978), and *Quel homme, quelle société?* (1978).

WALTER HEIM was born in Goldach (St Gallen) in 1922. He is a member of the Bethlehem Missionary Society, Immensee. He received his doctorate in *Volkskunde* (the study of popular beliefs and customs) from the University of Zürich. Between 1957 and 1974 he taught at a secondary school in Immensee. He was press officer to the 1972 Synod of the Diocese of Chur and has himself worked as a journalist, contributing articles on the missions. He has researched extensively into the changes in popular religious belief and practice since the Second World War, and has published his findings in many books and articles.

JOHN KILGALLEN, SJ, was born in Chicago, Illinois, in 1934 and ordained a Jesuit priest in 1965. He has degrees in classical studies, in philosophy and theology and, from the Pontifical Biblical Institute in Rome, a doctorate of Sacred Scripture. He is currently Associate Professor in the Department of Theology at Loyola University of Chicago. He has published *The Stephen Speech* (Analecta Biblica 67) (Rome, 1976); he has also written articles in journals of scripture.

WILLIAM McCREADY was born in Chicago, Illinois, in 1941. He is a senior study director at the National Opinion Research Center at the University of Chicago. Among his works are *The Ultimate Values of the American Population*.

ROLAND E. MURPHY, O Carm, was born in 1917 in Chicago, is an American Carmelite and a member of the editorial board of *Concilium*. He is professor of Old Testament studies at the Duke University Divinity School in Durham and is author of several articles and books dealing with the Old Testament.

JEAN RÉMY was born in Soumange, Belgium, in 1928. He is now a professor in the Faculty of Political and Social Sciences at the University of Louvain, and director both of the Centre de Recherche Socio-Réligieuse and of the Centre de Sociologie Urbaine et Rurale there. He has published many books of political economy and religious sociology.

JOHN SHEA teaches theology at St Mary of the Lake Seminary at Mundelein, Illinois, and is the director of the doctor of ministry at the Archdiocese of Chicago. He is the author of five books and of numerous articles in *Chicago Studies*, *The Ecumenist*, *Commonweal*, and *The Notre Dame Journal of Education*. He is presently investigating the ways of doing theological reflection within ministerial situations.

RUDOLF J. SIEBERT was born in Frankfurt a.M., Germany in 1927. He has studied theology, philosophy, history and philology in Germany and the U.S.A., and has taught in both countries. Since 1965 he has been professor of religion and society in the Department of Religion of Western Michigan University in Kalamazoo, Michigan.

TERESA A. SULLIVAN is assistant professor of sociology at the University of Chicago, and a faculty research associate at the Population Research Center. The focus of her research interests is minority groups and marginal workers.

DAVID TRACY was born in 1939 in Yonkers, New York. He is a priest of the diocese of Bridgeport, Connecticut, and a doctor of theology of the Gregorian University, Rome. He is professor of philosophical theology at the Divinity School of Chicago University. He is the author of *The Achievement of Bernard Lonergan* (1970) and *Blessed Rage for Order: New Pluralism in Theology* (1975). He contributes to several reviews and is editor of the *Journal of Religion* and of the *Journal of the American Academy of Religion*.